The Journeys of

Irish Street Preacher an...

History and H...

Compiled and Edited by

John K Bergland

Robert Williams

Lay Preacher in Ireland and Circuit Rider in America
First Methodist to preach in Virginia and North Carolina
First Methodist Printer and Publisher in America
Founder of the Norfolk and Petersburg Societies 1772
Founder of the Brunswick Circuit 1773-1774
Founder of Jerusalem United Methodist Church 1773

xulon
PRESS

Bishop Francis Asbury
First American Bishop

Asbury preached Williams funeral
"No person in America has awakened more souls
than has Robert Williams."
September 26, 1775

Introduction

R obert William's birth, baptism, and conversion are not documented. Neither is his call to preach. His travel journals, if there were any kept, have never been found. At John Wesley's conference of preachers which met at Leeds in 1766, Mr. Williams was appointed to the "North East Circuit," Ireland. In 1767 he was sent to the "Castlebar Circuit," Ireland, and returned to the same circuit in 1768. Before the Conference which met in August 1769, he sailed for America with his friend Thomas Ashton who paid for his passage..

Wesley was in Ireland from March 21 to July 24 in 1769. He had a sustained relationship with Robert Williams and referred to him as one of his "Helpers." John Wesley's journal expresses some dissatisfaction with three Irish lay preachers. He objected to Robert Williams preaching against Anglican clerics. He was unsympathetic with the unordained Robert Strawbridge taking liberty to baptize and serve communion. To John King, referring to his preaching, he said, "Scream no more at peril to your soul."

Arriving in the colonies before Boardman and Pilmoor, who were the appointed missionaries to America, Williams preached at John Street Church in New York. He served there in September and October of 1769. He was in Philadelphia and visited Pilmoor. He served with Captain

Webb in New Jersey. In Maryland he rode the circuits of Robert Strawbridge. He formed the first society in Virginia at Norfolk. The conferences of 1773 and 1774 list his appointments as Petersburg and the Brunswick Circuit.

Between 1769 and 1775 John Wesley sent eight missionaries to the American colonies. Richard Boardman, Joseph Pilmoor, Francis Asbury, Richard Wright, Thomas Rankin, George Shadford, Martin Rodda and James Dempster. When the Revolutionary War began all except Asbury had returned to England. Three Irish lay preachers, not officially appointed by Wesley, Strawbridge, Williams and King also remained in America.

That Robert Williams was an anointed servant of the Word has been made clearly evident by the Methodist churches that have grown up along the circuits he created. He, like the others, preached out of conviction. "Convictional preaching" is prompted by devotion to the gospel rather than being occasioned by a Sunday morning service.

Williams married in 1774 or 75.and died at his home between Norfolk and Suffolk in 1775 Bishop Asbury presided and preached at his funeral.

Methodism on the Roanoke

T he area now called Bracey began to form as a community in 1762 when a ferry across the Roanoke River (now
Lake Gaston) began operation. The territory around the northern
landing grew into a commercial center. This landing (Blanton's
Ferry)) became the town of Saint Tammany It was the first incor-
porated town in Mecklenburg County Virginia established by the
General Assembly.

In 1692, William Penn was granted land holdings in the
New World by King Charles II of England, He established a
new colony. As a Quaker, Penn believed in equality, respect, and
honor towards everything and everyone. He therefore arranged to
purchase the lands from the Indians. This attitude of respect ele-
vated William Penn's standing among the Delaware, especially
Chief Tammany of the Lenape Tribe.. Tammany's name means
"easy to talk to."

He and William Penn visited each other's homes, shared in
feasts and traded goods. In 1683, Tammany served as one of the
signers of the deed for the land that became Pennsylvania. He
made his mark on the deed in the form of a coiled snake. His
words became the credo of colonists like Franklin and Jefferson.
*"We shall live together in friendliness and helpfulness. But, I will
protect what is mine!*: "St. Tammany" became the name of a
secret colonial group that championed independence.

The trade area of St. Tammany (patron saint of American Liberty) covered a large region on both the north and south sides of the Roanoke River, at least as far east as the Brunswick County line and at least as far west as Flat Creek.

The road north of the landing, toward Petersburg, Virginia became known as St. Tammany Road. It ran through Dinwiddie County and Bath Parish where the Anglican priest, Devereaux Jarrat welcomed the Methodist circuit rider, Robert Williams, in 1772.

The road on the south side of the river ran through St. Tammany Plantation and near the neighboring plantation of Ebenezer Coleman where Williams preached under a giant oak tree. Jerusalem United Methodist Church was established in that place in 1773.

The Merrymount Plantation on the south side of the Roanoke was noted for exceptional horses. Robert William's horse was outstanding and much admired by Colonel Davis who owned Merrymount. A foal born in 1774 was named *Polly Williams*. This fine mare, never beaten in a match race, became a legend in the Roanoke Valley. The circuit riders preached against horse racing and cock fighting.

The Conference in Philadelphia in 1774 lists William's appointment as Petersburg Society. That year he put in place 26 preaching places along the Roanoke River Valley. They were known as the Brunswick Circuit. Rejoicing in the response to the "Awakening" Williams rode two hundred miles to a quarterly conference to report to Bishop Asbury that 200 hundred members had been added.

At the time of Williams' death September 26, 1775, Asbury said "No man in America has awakened more souls for Christ then has Robert Williams."

Sources and References

"A History of the M. E. Church, Vol. I" by Nathan Bangs
"History of the M. E. Church, Vol. I," by Abel Stevens,
"Cyclopedia of Methodism, 1882 Fifth Edition,"
by Matthew Simpson
"Autobiography and correspondence of Devereux Jarratt,
Anglican Priest Bath Parish"
"The Lost Chapters of Early Methodist History" Wakely
"Statistical History of Religion in America" C.C. Goss
"The Irish Palatines" The Methodist Review 1906
"Life on the Roaring Roanoke" Bracey
Historical records of Jerusalem United Methodist Church
Legends and Stories from old St. Tammany Road

Robert Williams whole history is full of interest. He was the apostle of Methodism in Virginia. Mr. Williams was the first Methodist minister in America who published a book, the first who married, the first whot located, and the first who died. He died in Virginia, the 26th of September, 1775. Bishop Asbury preached his funeral sermon, and pronounced over him a splendid eulogy. There is no monument to mark the place where this Methodist traveling minister, who found a grave in America,, is sleeping. Rev. Joseph Beaumont. Wakely

Section I

Early Methodist History

Related to

The Life and Legends
Of
Robert Williams
Born c. 1733
Died September 26, 1775

Founder of Jerusalem
United Methodist Church 1773

The Robert William's Oak

In 1772 news spread along the south side of the Roanoke River that a Methodist circuit rider was going to preach under the big willow oak on Ebenezer Coleman's plantation. A crowd gathered and Robert Williams preached with power. The oak tree became a regular preaching place on his Brunswick Circuit. In 1773 the Jerusalem United Methodist Church was formed.

Jerusalem United Methodist Church

As the apostle of Methodism in both Virginia and North Carolina, and through the conversion and work of Jesse Lee, Robert Williams' ministry influenced the founding of Methodism in New England and all across the colonies. William Watters, the first person born in American to become a Circuit Rider, and Philip Gatch, the second, were converted, shaped and called to convictional preaching by Robert

Williams. The power of Williams' ministry may be discerned in the Awakening Revival that began on Brunswick Circuit.

William's ministry in America was brief, but it was broad and deep. He is remembered by the faithful of Jerusalem as their founder. The "**Robert William's Tree,**" stood for centuries on the Coleman and Perkinson farm. It measured 26 feet around when it fell in 2007. This old preaching place for circuit riders still gathers the homecoming crowds of Jerusalem United Methodist Church

Wesley in Ireland

On the 9th day of August, 1747, John Wesley sailed across the Irish Sea from Holyhead. It took twenty six hours to make the sixty miles journey to Dublin's River Liffey. This was the first of his twenty-one visits. *(He was in Ireland in the summer of 1769 when Robert Williams, one of his Irish street preachers and the Methodist leader Thomas Ashton sailed for America).*

John Wesley's host for this first visit was William Lunell, a respected banker and cloth merchant. He was a Huguenot but also a member of the new Methodist Society in Ireland.

Wesley arrived on a Sunday morning and preached that afternoon at Evensong in St Mark's Church where he found "as gay and senseless a congregation as ever I saw."

Next day he rode out ten miles to meet with Archbishop Cobbe who had made serious objections to the Methodists preaching in any churches under his care or even in the open air. He considered them to be untrained for the work. Wesley argued that they were as surely called to preach as either of them. The Archbishop did not agree.

Soon great persecution began. The apprentices to the weaving trade in the Liberties of Dublin led the riots. When Methodism reached Cork, the persecution continued. "No man is fit to be a preacher here who is not prepared to die at any moment" wrote one of Wesley's lay preachers.

Still, Wesley persevered. "Have patience with Ireland and she will repay you," he declared. Time has proved him right. The Methodist Society among the Paletines in Co. Limerick sent forth Philip Embury and Barbara Heck, founders of the first Methodist Society in America. Robert Strawbridge, who built the first Methodist chapel in Maryland, and Captain Webb who helped build St. Georges in Philadelphia came from this society of Irish Methodists. Robert Williams, a Paletine, came from Ireland in 1769 and became the apostle of Methodism in Virginia and North Carolina.

The Irish Palatines

"In Co. Limerick, Wesley preached to the Palatines, German Protestant refugees who had been allowed to settle there a generation before. The Methodist doctrine and order took hold upon them, and from among them went out Philip Embury and Barbara Heck, who, with Robert Strawbridge, another native of Ireland, were to plant Methodism in New York and Maryland, and open the way for the widest extension of Methodism."

Quoted from Center for Wesley Studies

The winter of 1709 was severe. Famine and cold weighed heavy on the families of Protestant refugees in the Lower German Palatinate. These devout and pious Christians, shaped by the teachings of Martin Luther, had come there seeking refuge from persecution. But now, repeated raids from France in the 17th century and the ravages of starvation, made these industrious farmers ready to consider the offers of free land in the American Colonies and Northern Ireland

The benefits of immigrating to America were spread widely through posters and pamphlets. People began to leave the Palatinate in search of a better life. A few of these Palatines were able to sail directly to America. An estimated 13,000 were brought across the English Channel to London. That was more than the city could support. Queen Anne arranged for three thousand to be sent to Dublin. Another three thousand went to the Colonies landing in New York and in North Carolina. *Source: Early Eighteenths Century Emigration by Walter Knittle 1937.*

Queen Anne along with owners of landed Irish estates wanted to increase the Protestant population. Irish Catholics wanted to hold their own. Conflict and persecution followed. Landowners, greedy for larger profit, raised the costs of renting the land and farming. Within three years two thirds of the Palatine settlers had returned to England or Germany.

Of the 250 families that remained in Ireland, more than 100 were settled on the estate of Sir Thomas Southwell at Castlematrix near Rathkeale in Co. Limerick. Of the Landlords who successfully managed to induce their allotment of Palatine immigrants to remain in rural Ireland, the most successful was Southwell. He took care of many of their initial needs at considerable personal expense. By 1714, Sir Thomas Southwell had settled about 130 families on his lands.

The castle was built as a fortress during the early 1400s by the 7th Earl of Desmond. In the early 1600's the castle was granted to the Southwell family who converted it into a manor house. He lived at Castle Matrix when he settled Palestine families on his estate.

It was required that the Palatines identify with Anglican religion and share responsibility for the parish. Care of the roads, care of the poor, support of the state church, and other social responsibilities were mandated by the Queen. The parish Vicar was a teacher for basic education of the children..

Palatines kept many of their German customs and protestant beliefs. They honored the scriptures both Old and New Testament. They resisted the authority of the Pope and the Holy Roman Empire. The teachings of pietism inclined them toward rules for daily living. They were open and responsive to Methodist preaching and teaching.

Philip Embury and Barbara Ruttle Heck, came to America in 1760. In 1766 they formed the first Methodist class in the Colonies. This class built the first Methodist Church, John Street in New York. A Methodist church in Ireland also honors their memory.

Embury & Heck Memorial Methodist Church, Ballingrane, Ireland

Built in 1766, it is the last remaining Methodist place of worship in the Rathkeale area. This is one of three churches built to serve the needs of the local Palatines, and is dedicated to the memories of Philip Embury and Barbara Heck.

Palatines who knew each other in Ireland and were bonded through the Methodist classes and societies in both Ireland and the American Colonies are Philip Embury, Paul and Barbara Heck, Captain Webb, Thomas Ashton, Robert Strawbridge, John Evans, Samuel Yeargain, Robert Williams, John King, John Dickens, and Andrew Yeargain.

The Norfolk Society
Monumental United Methodist Church History
By Margaret Windley, Historian

W illiam Watters, the first American-born Methodist circuit rider, came to Portsmouth in 1772 with Robert Williams. He was only 21 years old, recently saved, and just getting used to becoming a Methodist minister. In 1773 he was received to preach in the conference.

In following years, he (Watters) alternated between "locating" and becoming active three or four times until he retired in 1805 due to poor health. He died in 1833.

William Watters left a journal like many other Methodist missionaries. And like so many other journals, he doesn't relate much about the environment. It's more of a record of his spiritual journey. However, during his missionary visit here, he recounted a few of Joseph Pilmore's Portsmouth sayings, referring to him as Mr. P.

The best-known Pilmore saying was that when he came up to get on the ferry boat, he was irritated by the ferry-men's cursing and exclaimed that if he had been brought there blindfolded, he would have known that he was "near Norfolk" because of the foul language.

Pilmore confided in his journal to a dislike of Williams but did not include Watters in the mention. Pilmore felt that Williams, an Irishman, disliked the English and preached against the Episcopal Church. Williams also had a unique preaching style of referring to angels and demons, which reportedly bothered people. Many people reportedly questioned his sanity. But he is credited with founding, among a long list of other churches, not only Monumental but also Emanuel and Jolliff.

Most people seemed to either appreciate Williams or to dislike him. Isaac Luke, the lay founder of Monumental, really seemed to think a lot of him. Williams put him in charge of a Methodist society that met in a warehouse in Gosport near the shipyard (source: letter of John W. H. Porter to the Norfolk District).

But there are two stories of Williams having problems with the mayor of Norfolk—once in 1769 and the other in 1772. It's tempting to think that the two separate accounts were just garbled versions of the same event. After all, did he really mount the steps to the Norfolk courthouse in 1769 and 1772 and both times sing the same hymn, "Come Ye Sinners to the Gospel Feast," to gain a crowd that turned unruly? Did the Norfolk mayor really make the same remark both times as he lined up a constable to arrest the preacher for attracting a crowd that responded violently to Williams' preaching?

In the 1772 account, Isaac Luke intervened and brought him home to Portsmouth where people would not dare to say anything to him. In the 1769 story, Williams went off with another person. But at least history indicates that Williams came both times. And other accounts point out that he had problems with crowd control.

Yeargain's Chapel on the Roanoke

A sketch of Yeargain's/ Chapel called
"Putting on Sunday Shoes".

Yeargain's Chapel was located in Bute County North Carolina on the north side of the Roanoke in the Pigeon Roost Creek area. Samuel Yeargain owned (since 1759) eleven hundred acres, on Little Pigeon Roost Creek, Pigeon Roost Creek, and Little Stone House Creek. At some point, probably in the early 1770's, Yeargain built a chapel on his plantation. (*We are indebted to Bebe Fox, a descendant of Samuel Yeargain for sharing this.*)

YEARGAN'S CHAPEL,
"PUTTING ON SUNDAY SHOES"

Bute Co. was formed from Granville Co. in 1764. Then in 1779 it was divided into Warren Co. and Franklin Co. Most of the records of Bute County are located in Warren Co. According to his travel diary, Bishop Asbury preached at the chapel on several occasions. He preached Robert Williams funeral service between Norfolk and Suffolk around the first of October in 1775. His travels took him to Yeargain's Chapel three times in November and December.

"Lord's day 5 November 1775. Rode about ten miles to Samuel Yeargain's Chapel, and met Brother George Shadford. My spirit was much united to him, and our meeting was like that of Jonathan and David." (In England, 1773, John Wesley had written to Shadford, "You must go down to Bristol...I let you loose, George, on the great continent of America. Publish your message in the open face of the sun, and do all the good you can.")

"Saturday 18 November 1775. I came to Samuel Yeargain's, a serious, sensible man. Lord's day 19. I began and ended the day with God. I had much liberty at the Chapel in discoursing on the subject matter, manner, and end of the apostles preaching."

"Lord's Day, 31 December 1775. Being the last day of the year, we held a watch-night at Samuel Yeargain's Chapel, beginning at six and ending at twelve o'clock. It was a profitable time, and we had much the power of God."

Andrew Yeargain, a Methodist Circuit rider in Virginia and North Carolina (Tar River Circuit) was a brother to Samuel. *[Will of SAMUEL YEARGAIN. 24 Dec.1784;__Meeting House & Chapel__ on part of home tract to be managed by MATTHEW MYRICK, NATHANIEL MASON & STEPHEN SHELL for public good. Extrs: FRANCIS JONES, *__JOHN DICKENS__*, NATHL.MASON & STEPHEN SHELL,Jr. Wit: EDMOND WEBB, <u>ANDREW YEARGAIN,Jr.</u> (Jurat) & GEORGE WEBB (Jurat).]*

John Dicken died from yellow fever (1798) in Philadelphia His will is recorded in both PA and in Halifax Co., NC (*where he once lived*). He was born in London, England (1746); was educated at Eton College, and came to America about 1772. In 1774 he began his ministry as a circuit preacher in Virginia and North Carolina. He is one of the founding fathers of Methodism in America; became the first married minister (he married Samuel Yeargain's daughter) to serve the John Street Church in New York;

went to Philadelphia where he organized the *Methodist* B*ook Concern*" He traveled the Brunswick Circuit along the Roanoke.

Robert Strawbridge House

Robert Strawbridge (? -1781) emigrated from Ireland to Frederick County, Maryland sometime between 1760 and 1766. A Methodist preacher in Ireland, he began preaching in Maryland soon after his arrival, making him the pioneer of Methodism on the American continent.

He preached in his log cabin home and began organizing Methodist societies as early as 1763 or 1764. The first class met in his home and soon a second met at a nearby home. John Evans (1734-1827), one of Strawbridge's converts, led the first class from 1768-1804. These were perhaps the earliest Methodist organizations in American history. During these early years, Strawbridge also built log meeting houses at Sam's Creek and Bush near Aberdeen.

Strawbridge soon began itinerating in Maryland, Pennsylvania, and Virginia, often preaching the first Methodist sermons heard in a settlement. He established a number of societies, prompted the construction of several Methodist chapels, possibly including the Old Stone Church in Leesburg, Virginia. He was tremendously popular and had a major influence on many young preachers.

Strawbridge, who was never ordained, nevertheless regularly administered the sacraments. At the first conference of Methodist preachers in America (1773), this practice was condemned, although an exception was made for Strawbridge, who was allowed to continue it under Asbury's direction. Francis Asbury in particular was unhappy about the matter, especially when Strawbridge ignored the conference's action and continued to administer the Lord's Supper as before!

Asbury recorded his frustration in his journal entry for June 24, 1774: "One of these letters informed me that Mr. Strawbridge was very officious in administering the ordinances. What strange infatuation attends that man! Why will he run before Providence?"

Section II

Story and Stories

History and Historical Fiction
by
John K Bergland

Growing Up Irish

"Robert Williams is a plain indefatigable (untiring) man."
Devereux Jarratt

The boy, Robert Williams was schooled by the local Vicar. He learned to read from the Bible; was taught Latin, history, geography and mathematics. As an apprentice he learned how to set type and print.

Irish stories and limericks surrounded him. But his special skill was with horses. All of the Irish Palatines were clever with horses. Robert Williams had a special way with them. He was driving a team and plowing straight furrows at age eleven.

Potatoes were the main crop in Ireland. Old ways of planting were with a shovel, bucket and rake. The Palatines brought better ways of farming. They plowed a furrow, fertilized it with dung (it took only a third as much), covered it and harrowed it with the help of horses. Most farm boys could drive a team.

Robert's father hired him out. He had run up a bill at the local tavern and couldn't pay it. At his weekly visit for a glass or two, the tavern keeper brought it up. "I can't serve you any more, my friend. Not until you have paid your tab." "Can I trade you some vegetables, butter and eggs for it," asked old Seth Williams. "Sure. But it won't be enough. You'll likely have to work it off."

"I can't do that" replied Seth. "My farming takes all my spare time every day. Let me suggest something else." And now young Robert Williams was about to be employed by a tavern.

"My oldest boy, Robert is about 14 and a fine strapping lad he is." "He's a willing worker; he's a fast learner, and he's quick and strong." "Maybe if he'd work for you without wages every afternoon, we could settle the account."

Robert Williams began washing glasses, sweeping floors and clearing tables on the inside of the tavern. Outside his job was to shovel up horse manure and take care of the stage coach teams.

He was sweeping the floors every afternoon and every afternoon he learned another Irish limerick. The taverns were wonderfully social and at times boisterous. They were always filled with a mixture of folks from drovers to merchants along with a crowd of locals. Shared "limericks were a favorite past time. One table would shout out and another would answer. Like this one.

"A mouse in the house woke Miss Dowd.
She was frightened—it must be allowed.
Soon a happy thought hit her—
To scare off the critter,
She sat up in bed and just meowed."

Irish laughter filled the whole room. Then another table shared a limerick.

"There was an old man of Nantucket,
Who kept all his cash in a bucket.
But, his daughter named Nan,
Ran away with a man.
And as for the bucket, Nan tuk it."

Robert Williams liked the third limerick he heard that day. It fit into one of his favorite Genesis stories.

"There was a sly lady of Eden,
Who on apples was quite fond of feedin'.
She gave one to Adam,
Who said, 'Thank you, Madame.'
And they both got kicked out of Eden."

Robert Williams—Stage Driver

One afternoon the stage rolled up in front of the tavern. When the last of the passengers got off, the stage driver, after a long day, wanted refreshment. "Just have Robert park your stage and tie up your horses," suggested the tavern owner. "Can he manage four spirited horses?" asked the driver. "That boy can drive that team through the eye of a needle," came the reply. So Robert Williams, sixteen, going on seventeen, gathered up the reins of a stage coach team and a new skill unfolded.

He managed the teams and the stages every afternoon. One day a driver said, "Robert Williams, we are needing a substitute driver for the stages. Why don't you come down to the staging yards and work with harnessing and fitting? You'll get plenty of time with some mighty good horses.

Then if you're needed you can fill in. I'd be pleased if you would ride with me some and learn the way of stage driving." Robert began working for wages. He still lived at home and paid for his keep. His mother and sisters still made his clothes. His father was making headway on the tavern debt.

Stage driving on difficult roads in all kinds of weather was demanding, but it was always an adventure. Williams thrived on it. One day a passenger from Dublin, who, because of his gracious manners, stood out from the rest, noticed Robert William's abilities. He introduced himself. "I'm Thomas Ashton from Dublin. Before that I was from County Limerick. Are you from Rathkeale?" he asked. "Then you probably remember my friends who are now in America. Philip Embury and his cousin, Barbara Heck."

"Yes I know them. They are about five years older than me. Left for the colonies in 1760.We used to go to hear Methodist preaching together. I don't think I saw you there though."

"No, not likely; I went off to Dublin and have been making my living there. The Lord has blessed me too." Thomas Ashton's father had come to Castle Matrix and through diligence; ingenuity and thrift established his own farm and farms. Like his father, Ashton had improved on all that was given him. He was in County Limerick to supervise his farms.

Thomas Ashton had been shaped by the teachings of John Wesley. Moreover, he was one to whom Wesley looked for his travel and hospitality needs when in Ireland. Wesley had sent word that he would be in Ireland for several weeks. Ashton agreed to provide for him.

Wesley would cross the Irish Sea on a Packet, a sailing vessel that carried the mails. He would dock at Dublin and preach in the area. Then he and Ashton were to take the stage to County Limerick. They intended to travel through the area, especially among the Palatines. There were good preaching houses, some churches, and many open air preaching places where the large crowds would gather.

"Robert Williams, can you arrange for a chaise and a fine team for John Wesley? Will you be our driver?" Thomas Ashton asked." I'll arrange for the cost of it with the stage company." The young stage driver knew exactly the team he wanted—a pair of gray's, quick and gentle and willing. They could go at a good pace for ten miles or even twenty if needed. When fresh they were a handful, but he welcomed the challenge.

From Limerick they set out along the Shannon River. It had rained during the night and the road was slippery. Robert chose to ride the lead horse. He had better control that way. Wesley's journal would tell about the fall. On the edge of a precipice where the road sloped a bit, the lead horse slipped and fell. The young horseman was underneath, and the second horse, still in the shafts of the chaise, reared up and was about to bolt.

Quick as a wink, Robert Williams was on his feet, bridles in hand and back in control. He looked over the edge to the river below and wondered if God's protecting hand had spared them, or was it Irish luck. He wanted to lighten the moment so he chose the latter. "If you are lucky enough to be Irish, you don't need any more luck at all," said Williams.

Time was when John Wesley had been more than a little afraid, but not these days. He always had a steady calm that unnerved others. With wonderful words of confidence and faith he said, "I would not speak of it as Irish luck. It is God who keeps me safe. He shelters us under the safety of his wings" Then he began to sing.

All praise to thee, my God this night
For all the blessings of the light
Keep me, O keep me King of kings,
Beneath thine own almighty wings.
Praise God, from whom all blessings flow,
Praise him, all creatures here below,
Praise him above, ye heavenly host,
Praise Father, Son, and Holy Ghost.

Three days into the journey, they came to the place that Wesley called the finest cathedral that ever gathered true worshippers. It was a ravine. Along one side there were gently sloping hillsides, green with new grass. There was space enough to accommodate more than three thousand. The soldiers had carved out a preaching place on the other side. Their presence kept the great crowd orderly. Wesley's text was, "Put on the whole armor of God. Take the shield of faith and the helmet of salvation!"

Perhaps more than anyone else in that great crowd, Robert Williams wanted to do just that.

John Wesley

Converted

As soon as Wesley's converts believed, *"they spake; salvation by faith being their standing topic"*

A s a boy Robert Williams had family and neighbors all around him. They knew him and sometimes knew him better than he knew himself. But like all folks, in challenging times he felt very much alone.

Listening to Wesley preach and captured by the serious, *close to the nerve style* of this holy man, RW was developing concerns that he had never had before. He wondered about the *"state of his soul."* He had heard talk about assurance of salvation. Now the question of being right with God had become a nagging worry. The words of the Charles Wesley Hymn kept ringing in his ears.

> How can we sinners know
> Our sins on earth forgiven?
> How can my gracious Savior show
> My name inscribed in heaven?
> We who in Christ believe
> That He for us hath died,
> We all His unknown peace receive
> And feel His blood applied.
> We by His Spirit prove
> And know the things of God,
> The things which freely of His love
> He hath on us bestowed.
> The Spirit of my God
> Hath certified Him mine,
> And all the tokens showed,
> Infallible, divine.

Robert William's soul struggle began. Some would say that he was "under conviction." Religious experience is deeply personal. This was an issue he would have to settle *alone*.

(The desert fathers taught that knowing God begins with "being alone with the Alone.")

The gift of solitude is silence. The gift of silence is prayer. The gift of prayer is faith. The gift of faith is love. The gift of love is God. God is love.

The most important happenings in one's life are experienced quite alone. You are born all alone. Your hungers are yours alone. So are your pains and your joys. You must die alone. Your believing is like your dying. You have to that alone too. "Alone with the Alone" is surely the way of it—the way of receiving the gift of faith and the assurance of salvation.

Have you ever heard the "Other Voice" speaking? It is the language of the boundary. Sometimes one does not only hear the words of scripture, the lyrics of a song, or the message of the preacher. Rather one hears an 'other voice' speaking. Saints have called it the "Mysterium Tremendum." It is a powerful silence. To have the "Other Voice" name you and call you is life changing.

Robert Williams never considered sad times in his boy hood to be "soul struggle" but he had done plenty of "con-templating." He had a favorite hiding place for times when he needed to sort things out. It was in the stable; up in the corner of the stall where the gray mare, Molly, stood eating hay. When he felt all alone, felt like an orphan in the world, he would slip up beside her, bury his face in her mane, and cry if he needed to.

Then he would whisper to her. Tell her things that he wouldn't say to anyone. He hardly told some of those things to himself. After a while he began to sense that the gray mare knew he was there. He was learning about the presence. He was beginning to experience the "Thou" of the otherness.

Some folks treat horses and cows and pigs and chickens just like they treat a rock or a rain barrel. Any conscious-ness and any awareness that those creatures may have is simply overlooked. Not so for Robert Williams. He liked being with the living. He liked being conscious. He even talked to the chickens.

One day he caught sight of a fox. It was ducked low and trotting along the course of a ditch. When the fox saw him it stopped dead in its tracks; looked hard at him. The hair stood up on its back. The hair stood up on Robert's neck too. He quickly said, "Hello Mr. Fox. Don't be afraid. Don't run away. Stay. Let's talk a bit." But quick as a flash the fox was gone.

The boy was awakened now, and filled with wonder. He wanted to know more about foxes. He wondered how much the fox knew about him. It's a hard thing to do — to talk to creatures different than we are. It is not easy to "get with" any creature, especially those different than ourselves. It is a good thing to try to hear the language of the boundary. It creeps in on you, more like awareness than sound.

Robert Williams learned early how to "get with a horse." He learned how they relaxed to his touch, quieted to his voice; gentled with his presence and quickened to his command. His ability to employ their language made him very good with horses. He watched; he waited; he listened. He opened himself up to their otherness.

Now Robert Williams, prompted by the power of this great man of God, John Wesley, wanted what he had. He wanted a personal knowledge of the saving grace proclaimed by this preacher. He wanted a word from God; a blessed word of assurance.

Wesley spoke often about his May 24, 1738 awakening at Aldersgate. While hearing the preface to the book of Romans read, he felt his heart *"strangely warmed."* He called it his conversion when "I knew my sins, *even mine own sins"* were forgiven. John Wesley said that if it had not been for that "one golden hour" there would have been no world-wide Methodism, and the eighteenth century would not have known the Great Awakening.

For several years Robert Williams had been gaining insight into Wesley's teaching. He was an apprentice in a print shop. Wesley wrote tracts and sermons that he would have printed. One time some of the type setting was assigned to Williams. As he labored over each letter in every word

on every line, the main points of Methodist doctrine were
burned into his soul.

Justification before God is by faith alone!
*(1.) All men and women are by nature, "dead in sin,"
and, consequently, "children of wrath."*
(2.) They must fear this wrath that is to come.
*(3.) They must flee from the wiles of Satan and put their
whole trust in Christ.*
(3.) Such faith produces inward and outward holiness.

For many of Wesley's converts the moment of belief was
also the moment of call. Like the prophet Isaiah records,
"I saw the Lord, High and lifted up and I heard Him say,
"Whom shall I send? Who will go for me?" I said, "Here
am I. Send me."

In a short time laymen became powerful servants of the
Word. Large crowds gathered where ever they preached.
They, along with their followers, were called Methodists. It
was not a new religion. They did not form a new church, but
rather established societies to revive the Church of England.

Robert Williams found a familiar praying place during
Wesley's sermon that day. He had stayed with the chaise and
the horses, ready to carry JW to his next preaching place. As
Wesley preached, Robert Williams heard the "Other Voice"
speaking. It was naming him; calling him. He stood next to
the lead horse, stroked his neck, buried his face in the mane,
and the old feelings of being with the "other" swept over
him. He felt the witness of the Spirit within. God's Spirit
bearing witness with his spirit that he was a child of God and
an heir with Christ.

After the preaching had ended, praises filled the valley.
John Wesley and his friend Ashton returned to the car-
riage where the driver was waiting. "Mr. Wesley," Robert
Williams said hesitantly, "May I tell you about an experience

I had today? It was during the time you were preaching to the great crowd down in the valley. I met the Lord!"

He really did not have to say much more. A radiance of faith and joy shone out of him.

John Wesley took his hand and at the same time touched his shoulder. He began to pray. The last words of his prayer were, "Father, Son and Holy Spirit, let your power fall mightily upon your servant, Robert Williams. Convince him of your steadfast love and grace. Make him a preacher of the gospel and a faithful servant of your Word."

Robert Williams knew he would never be the same again. Jesus Christ was now his hope and his salvation. He gladly named him as his Lord. For the next three years he would be a lay preacher in Ireland. The Conferences at Leeds in 1766, 67 and 68 would determine where he would labor.

Come Over and Help Us

John Wesley came to Colonial America in 1739 as the Anglican priest of Oglethorpe's colony. He came intending to serve the religious needs of the settlers and evangelize the Indians. By his own witness he was a failure. "I came to convert sinners, but who will convert me?"

At Aldersgate his "heart warming" experience radically changed him. He became convinced by grace, prevenient grace, justifying grace, sanctifying grace. His preaching changed dramatically. Convictional preaching, convinced and convincing, became his style. The prophet Jeremiah described it. The Word "burned like fire in his bones."

The Anglican Church in Great Britain was state owned and state supported. Residents in each parish were required by law to support and attend the church. It was the same in the American Colonies. The governors provided funding for three things in every new settlement—a court house and stockade, a chapel, and a musket for each household. The rector's salary was paid by the state.

John Street meeting house in New York City was not considered a church. They built a fireplace in it so that it qualified as a dwelling. New church buildings, that were not Anglican, were not given building permits. Non Anglicans were considered to be dissenters.

Convictional preaching was the style of lay preachers like Robert Williams and Philip Embury. No one paid them to preach. Embury was a carpenter. But the society in New York wanted clergy who would devote all of their time to the care of souls. They were so committed to the cause that they were willing to under write the support of their meeting house and their preachers.

Thomas Taylor, one of John Street (Wesley Chapel) members, appealed to Mr. Wesley for the appointment of preachers. He asked for those "whose heart and soul are in the work," saying that they would even sell their coats to secure the cost. The letter was dated April 11, 1768. No one volunteered for the mission that year.

(*In September and October of 1769 Robert Williams was John Street first paid preacher. Not only did the society pay his salary, they also bought his cloak, his hat, his stockings, his chest and provided for the keep of his horse.*)

The following year, 1769, after John Wesley's challenging sermon to his preachers, Boardman and Pilmoor accepted the challenge. Boardman was appointed to John St. in New York. Pilmoor was appointed to St. Georges in

Philadelphia. It was an official appointment. The conference paid their passage, sent 50 pounds to be applied to the debt on John Street. JW sent along some of his sermons and tracts. Before they set sail, Robert Williams came on his own.

There was also a Methodist meeting house in Maryland. Robert Strawbridge, an Irish Paletine farmer, was a persuasive lay preacher. In 1764 he built a log meeting house at Sam's Creek and was spreading biblical holiness throughout the whole region. John Evans, and other Irish immigrants, associated with Strawbridge, entreated their old Irish neighbors in Co. Limerick to join them in America. They especially wanted effective preachers.

One day Thomas Ashton was in the company of Robert Williams. He had a document granting him 2500 acres of land in New York State and also a letter from Maryland. "Robert," he began, "Do you remem*mbe*r what those ancient Greeks wrote to St. Paul when they wanted him to join them in the cause of Christ? It was, *"come over into Macedonia and help us."*

Ashton gave the Irish lay preacher a letter he had received from John Evans. The class meeting that began in his house had grown mightily. The Methodists were gaining followers throughout Maryland and northern Virginia. "Robert Williams, I'm going to America "Ashton said."I want to settle on the land I have been given. Why don't you come with me? I'll pay your passage and if you'll preach the Methodist Way in the colonies it will be good for all of us."

"Listen for the call of God, my friend Maybe you'll hear the same words—*come over and help us*. We can land in New York. Philip Embury and Paul Heck will meet us and help us get settled. Embury has been wanting a preacher at John Street, and no one has volunteered to go"

On that day an Irish vender, street preacher and apprentice printer, through the pretty ways of providence, was claimed for a new ministry. Robert Williams was destined to become an apostle of Methodism in America and especially in Virginia and North Carolina

Joe Froggers

A couple known as Aunt Crease and Black Joe lived at the edge of a pond in Marblehead, Massachusetts. In early May they would open their house as a local tavern. They served grog (rum diluted with water.). Joe would play the fiddle and Aunt Crease would cook.

One of her specialties was a molasses cookie the size of a lily pad. She made them for sailors, who found they stored well in barrels during long sea voyages. The rum was key to that. Square riggers would stock up on Joe Froggers before making a crossing of the Atlantic.

At the end of May, a time when frogs were peeping in the pond, many of the ships would set sail for England. Sailors came to get Joe's plate sized cookies. They associated them with the lily pads in the frog pond. That's why the cookies were called Joe's Froggers. Over time the possessive was dropped, and the name became Joe Froggers.

The recipe became legend. Molasses cookies made with rum were not native to the Irish, but they were so well suited as fare for long ocean voyages that they soon found their way to the carts of venders at the Irish harbors. Salt pork, sauer kraut and hard tack were foods that kept well in the storage barrels on the square riggers. Joe Froggers kept well too and were a welcome change in a sea farers diet. .

This recipe will yield 8 dozen. Be sure to use the specified ingredients — no substitutions. Avoid too much rolling out.

- 3/4 cup hot water
- 1/4 cup plus 1 tablespoon dark rum
- 1 cup (2 sticks) butter
- 2 cups sugar
- 2 teaspoons baking soda
- 2 cups dark molasses
- 6 to 7 cups flour
- 1 tablespoon salt
- 1-1/2 teaspoons ginger
- 1 teaspoon cloves
- 1 teaspoon allspice
- 1/2 teaspoon freshly grated nutmeg

Combine hot water and rum in small bowl. In large bowl, cream together butter and sugar. In a third bowl, combine soda and molasses. In a fourth bowl, combine 6 cups flour with salt and spices. Blend water and rum into creamed mixture in large bowl. Add molasses and dry ingredients alternately; blend. (If dough is too stiff, add a little water; if not stiff enough, add more flour.) Divide dough into three balls, cover with plastic wrap, and cool thoroughly. Preheat oven to 375 degrees F. Sprinkle board with remaining flour. Roll out dough and cut with 3-inch cookie cutter or rim of glass bowl. Bake on greased cookie sheet 10 minutes.

Robert Williams was not only an Irish street preacher. He was also a vender. He had long experience in trading vegetables for old clothes, old clothes for books and books for money.

After he had sold his horse and paid his debts, he had a few left overs to barter. He got a loaf of bread, a jug of milk and then came upon a small barrel of Joe Froggers.

A tavern keeper had told him about mixing rum and water to make grog. After a month at sea, the drinking water in barrels became foul. Sailors were rationed a half pint of rum per day to make the water drinkable. Williams, although opposed to drink and drunkenness, yielded to the preservative function of rum. He reasoned that these *Joe Froggers*, laced with rum, would serve well on the crossing.

Thomas Ashton paid their passage and two Irish Methodists sailed from Limerick for the American Colonies. Ashton wanted to settle on the patent, (free land) that he had been assigned along the Hudson in New York State. Williams would begin his ministry in the colonies at John Street church which Philip Embury had begun in New York City. The Atlantic crossing would take at least six weeks.

"If you want to learn to pray, go to sea"
Herbert 17th century poet

For ten days it had been smooth sailing. Then, one evening, the Captain said, "We're in for a bit of blow. Those clouds gathering north of us will bring a storm. It'll give us a good push if we can keep the sails up for a little bit. Stormy winds can speed up the crossing."

Robert Williams slept uneasily that night. At first light he left the lower deck and went top side. The waves looked like mountains. Already the sails were tied to the cross beams and sailors were busy securing barrels and chests. The crates for the fowl were being covered with canvas or taken below deck.

"Can I be of any help? Williams asked the first mate. "Sure! And we're more than grateful. Be careful though. Hang on to something. Tie down everything. And don't slip on this wet deck."About that time a sailor lost his footing and went sliding under the chicken coops. It was a messy place. "Clean yourself up later son," the mate said. "Now just keep on task!'

Turning to the Methodist preacher the mate said, "It's always good to have a man of God on board. The crew is a whole lot less afraid. Sailors believe that they can survive any storm with a holy man among them. Except maybe if he's a Jonah" *Jonah had been commanded by God, "Go to Ninevah and cry out against its wickedness." The prophet didn't want to preach to those pagans. He took a boat headed in the opposite direction. A storm threatened to sink the ship.* "You're not running away from God are you?" asked the mate. "No, not running from God at all" said Williams. "In fact I'm going to the cities in America to cry out against their wickedness."

"We're going to be alright, and you are too" said the mate. "By the way, Mr. Williams, I sure do thank you for that Joe Frogger you gave me last evening. Best molasses cake on the sea! Your barrel is among those over there. Make sure it's tied tight."

Don't Ever Sell Your Saddle
Life's a Long, Long Ride

W hen Robert Williams sold his horse to pay his debts, he kept his saddle. His saddle bags held four books—the Bible, a hymn book, a church book and a pocket book. When he arrived in America his pocket book was empty. He stepped onto the dock in New York City penniless. Williams was always resourceful and before long he would be taking care of himself. He would find a way so that no one would need to care for him. But as for now, he welcomed help from his friends who were also friendly to the gospel.

The John Street Meeting would pay a monthly salary. They bought him a cloak, beaver top hat and three pairs of long stockings. His britches and trousers were in satisfactory condition. The first big expense for a traveling preacher was the cost of a horse.

People moved around the colony by foot, wheeled vehicle, horse, or small boat. The least expensive and most common way to get from one place to another was by foot. Walking was the common mode of transportation. .

Stage wagons offered public transportation along city routes and between nearby towns. Water travel was another way to get around. Along the rivers, every plantation had a dock.

Ships were the only method of transportation across the Atlantic. The voyage from England to the American Colonies took an average of six to eight weeks. Ships also sailed along the coast between ports such as Boston, New York, Philadelphia, Norfolk, or Charleston. Smaller boats navigated the major rivers throughout the colonies. Often it was easier to travel by water than by land.

A horse was worth 3 chickens, 2 pigs, and a dairy cow. Even poor folks in the colonies purchased a horse and saddle as soon as they could afford them. Horses sold for as little as £5, but a registered horse cost as much as £500.

The folks at St John's knew where Robert Williams could get a registered saddle horse. But all was not so good. The horse could not be ridden—yet. Out near the Staten Island Barracks of the British soldiers, there was stallion that had been stabled by an officer. He never came back to claim him. The rumor was that he couldn't control the animal.

Broadsides, advising any interested party with rights to the horse to come forward, were printed and posted. There was no response. Robert Williams could legally claim the horse, but he would need to get it under control. If this stallion had ever been gentled, he surely didn't stay gentle.

"What a beautiful stallion." Williams remarked when he first saw him. "He's well bred and suited for traveling. He has spirit. He's mighty bold and independent." Matthew 5:5 says, "Blessed are the meek." The horse needed to be a bit more meek. But the stallion never would be gentle if that meant *meek like a mouse.* Maybe he could be shaped into the kind of gentleness (meekness) honored by the Lord. Aristotle's dictionary references the Greek word for "meekness" in the Beatitudes as like unto a gentle horse; *"Always angry at the right time: Never angry at the wrong time."*

There were two mares in the pasture with the stallion. When the men approached, the horse stepped boldly into the space between the mares and the visitors. He lifted his head high. "Ah! Look at that, will ya?" said RW. "That horse is bold; and he's *'angry at the right time.'* Now we'll need to shape him a bit so he's *never angry at the wrong time.*"

A month later a gray stallion, called Traveler, was turning heads on the streets of New York City and along the Hudson River. So was his rider; a tall broad shouldered Irishman, with cloak, top hat and Bible, on the way to some preaching place.

Most colonists had some type of vehicle. Farmers found carts and wagons useful. These conveyances hauled produce to market and carried families to church. Wealthier individuals bought a riding chaise, a buggy. A new lightweight two-wheeled buggy cost £10 to £45. A used chaise cost as little as £2.

Robert Williams bought a good used chaise and trained his horse to pull it. Traveling between settlements and cities, Williams used the buggy. It could carry his chest; the books and tracts he had to give away or sell, and his printing supplies. Where roads were not maintained or where there were only trails, the circuit rider always rode.

Come Before Winter
Off to the Battenkill and then to Maryland

Methodist circuit riders were proverbial for having good horses,

After building St John.s Church and parsonage, Philip Embury wanted to build a house on the Embury patent (free land) in Washington County. Embury and Thomas Ashton had both been given land grants in upstate New York. Each had 2500 acres available to him. Their holdings were separated by the Battenkill River. New York City was too confining for the carpenter preacher Philip Embury. He was ready to move north.

Robert Williams was well placed in New York. It was a good place for a street vender. Upon arriving he became the preacher at John Street. His ministry would be for a two month period. Richard Boardman, Wesley's assigned preacher, would arrive from England in late October and would assume the appointment.

From the beginning Williams was "willing to travel." That was the style of his Lord. He accepted the call to itinerant ministry, and the society at John Street was willing to equip him for it. The appointments of circuit riders were usually six months and seldom more than a year.

Thomas Ashton and Philip Embury were about to explore the territory in upstate New York. They had learned that there were already Irish Palatines settled in that neighborhood The evening before they were to leave New York, these old friends from Ballingrane began to reminisce about former neighbors in Ireland. They discussed Washington County, the settlers near Salem and their friend Robert Strawbridge in Maryland. Robert Williams only listened.

"Which side of the river is your land on, Philip?" Thomas Ashton asked.

"It is north and west," replied Embury. "Where are your holdings?."

"I've studied the map and I'm inclined to believe that I'll be across the river from you." said Ashton. "Wouldn't it be wise to look at both land grants, but just settle one at first. Twenty five hundred acres is big county." "I need for at least three families to settle on my land. That's what the contract reads. You and yours could be one of them," continued Ashton.

"Robert Williams, take a look at this survey," suggested Philip Embury, wanting to include the younger man in the conversation. "You're good at map reading. What's the best way to get there?"

RW suggested a route on the east side of the Hudson River. He began tracing it from Staten Island in New York City.

The conversation about the route along the Hudson turned into talk about the Battenkill River. It's not a big river. It is born in the Green Mountains and flows for about 50 miles before finally reaching the Hudson. The springs that feed it keep the water cool The Battenkill is famous for trout fishing. *(Headquarters for Orvis fly fishing enterprises are situated on the banks of the Batten Kill. The beauty and history behind this region makes a trip here worthwhile.)*

Philip Embury had gone to the area several times during his almost 10 years in America. His descriptions of the beauty of the river and mountains were captivating. His enthusiasm for the place was contagious.

"You make it sound like the Crystal River in heaven; the one that flows by the throne of God," observed Robert Williams "I sure hope that there are some fish in it."

"I don't know about the Crystal River," Chuckled Philip Embury. "But I do know there are fish in the Battenkill. One evening I came upon a friendly Indian who had a fine catch. He gave us enough for our supper." *(For contemporary fly fishermen: try a Tungsten Prince Nymphs, no weight and a 6X tippet. Creep up carefully and fish every little seam.)*

Two months later in early November, Robert Williams decided to visit his friend, Thomas Ashton. He mounted his horse Traveler and set out to find him. After a short visit on the Battenkill, there was a longer journey waiting.

He had a letter in his saddle bags. It was from Robert Strawbridge with greetings from his wife Elizabeth, old friends from the Methodist Society among the Palatines in Ireland.

Dear Robert Williams, It is a great encouragement to me to know that you are in America, and that you are preaching in New York. I rejoice, to learn about the ways in which God is using you. Never be ashamed to testify for our Lord.

There is a field "white unto harvest' here in Maryland. If it is ever possible for you to do so, please come and help me on the circuits.

PS If you still peddle old cloths, please bring me a cloak. Like St Paul wrote to Timothy, "Bring my cloak. Do your best to come before winter."2 Timothy 4:21

Old Clothes

As a street vender in Ireland, Robert Williams mastered the fine art of bartering. When he came from the farm to the city, his cart was usually loaded with vegetables— cabbages, potatoes, beets and beans. As an experienced apprentice in printing, Williams also had used books, blank record books, tracts and stationary articles, especially news papers to sell. When interested buyers had no money, he was willing to barter. "What do you have to trade?" he would ask.

One available, tradable and easy to sell item was used clothing. In London, Dublin and New York, the cry "Ol cloths! Ol' cloths!" was heard often in the streets. Irish and Jewish immigrants were involved in the enterprise.

> "The peddler passed the house today,
> And gave his call in his plaintive way
> "Ol' clothes! Ol' clothes! Ol' clothes!
> Any ol' clothes to trade away?
> I searched the house and made a heap,
> Of things that I didn't want to keep.
> Old unused garments and well read books,
> Clothes that just hung on closet hooks,
> Where dust would gather and moths would chew,
> It was time for the old to make way for new.

The small salary RW was paid at John Street Church would end along with the appointment, when Richard

Boardman arrived in November. The enterprising Williams went into the city everyday. His cart was loaded with fresh vegetables, stationary, Bibles, tracts, used books and used clothing. The clothes had been cleaned and repaired.

Robert Williams didn't go to the street markets. Instead he went to the fine residential areas to make his pitch. With horse and buggy he drove through the street ringing a bell and calling out, "Old clothes! Old clothes!" He kept his eyes focused on the street level windows. That's where the servants would be. He saw a window raise and a pretty Irish girl wave and beckon. Williams turned on his Irish charm. "Ah! Look at you lass. I do believe you are the prettiest sight these old eyes have seen in years," The maid tried to ignore the flattery. But she did like it. "Do you have need for fresh vegetables? RW asked."Have you any old clothes to be rid of?"

The servant girl had some men's used clothing, two pair of used boots, and a stack of books. The potatoes and cabbages were not enough to match their worth. RW had some writing paper, a new "Poor Richard's Almanac" and several used books. The conversation was warm and friendly and the exchange was agreeable. Williams would trade the clothes again. Some of them would be taken to his tailor friend who would clean and repair them. He hung them on his racks to sell. He paid Robert Williams real money.

Type Setting and Printing

Paper was scarce in the colonies and paper mills were few. The paper mills supported the old clothes industry too. Rags of all kinds were soaked and boiled and beaten into the pulp used to make paper. Rag picking was the low end of the old clothes business. Benjamin Franklin was a "rag picker" in London when he found himself penniless. Robert Williams did some "rag picking" in New York City.

On his way to Maryland Williams traveled through Philadelphia. A classified ad for a used printing press had captured his attention. He was happily surprised to learn that it was owned by Benjamin Franklin. Their conversation ranged from printing to paper making to rag picking and to traveling preachers. Franklin had been mightily impressed by the preaching of George Whitfield. Now this Methodist circuit rider, Robert Williams was earning his respect.

Robert Williams lacked sufficient funds to buy the printing materials out right. Franklin agreed to let him peddle his Pennsylvania Gazette and sell his almanacs for a part of the payment. He was interested in some excellent books and Wesley sermons that Robert Williams had. He wanted the itinerant preacher to have a map and survey of the Roanoke Valley. It had been made by Thomas Jefferson's father Peter. A supply of new papers and almanacs greatly enriched the Irish peddler's inventory.

"Do you have a good Irish blessing to leave with me Mr. Williams? Franklin asked.

"Yes I do. Indeed I do," he answered The Irish preacher always had a ready limerick.

> May love and laughter light your days,
> and warm your heart and home.
> May good and faithful friends be yours,
> wherever you may roam.
> May peace and plenty bless your world
> with joy that long endures.
> May all life's passing seasons
> bring the best to you and yours!

Benjamin Franklin handed him a copy of the latest "Poor Richard's Almanac." It was filled with good counsel and wise sayings. Sensitive to the short lives of Methodist circuit riders, Mr. Franklin noted:

Wish not so much to live long as to live well.
Those who would give up essential liberty
To purchase a little temporary safety
Deserve niether liberty or safety.

Aware of Irish tempers he marked another.

Take it from Richard, poor and lame,
What begins in anger, ends in shame.

Pilmoor was in Philadelphia at St. Georges. Robert Williams went by to see him. Wesley had authorized RW to preach in America under the supervision of. Pilmoor. He did not have any work for him. Williams offered to print notices and sermons for him. Then he told him of his intention to go to Maryland where, along with the Irish doctor, John King, he would preach on the circuits of Robert Strawbridge. These were expanding every day.

Apostle to Virginia

Robert Williams Preached on the steps of
the Norfolk Court house
He formed the Norfolk Society in 1772

As the first of the British colonies in America, Virginia was also the largest and most prosperous. Virginia provided four of the first five presidents of the United States — Washington, Jefferson, Madison and Monroe. They were the planters of great plantations in the Tidewater area, like Mt Vernon and Monticello. All of these great men were slave owners and gentry. Slavery was the primary key to the wealth of the state. Norfolk was Virginia's largest sea port. There were an estimated 200,000 slaves in Virginia at the time of the Revolution.

The capital city of Williamsburg was the only place in Virginia that had a newspaper until the eve of the American Revolution. William Parks published the first issue of the Virginia Gazette in Williamsburg on 6 August 1736 and continued this weekly until it was moved to Richmond in 1774.

On 9 June 1774, William Duncan began publishing a weekly newspaper in Norfolk. This was the first Virginia newspaper to be printed outside of Williamsburg. Duncan and his successor, John Hunter Holt, issued the Norfolk Intelligencer until 20 September 1775 when the royal governor of Virginia, the Earl of Dunmore confiscated the printing press.

There was a distinction between gentle and simple folk in Virginia that also prevailed in England Devereux Jarratt, the Virginia born Anglican priest of Petersburg writes, "We were accustomed to look upon, what were called **gentle folks**, as beings of a superior order. I was quite shy of them, and kept off at a humble distance. A periwig, in those days, was a distinguishing badge of **gentle folk**. When I saw a man riding the road, near our house, with a wig on, it would so alarm my fears, and I would run off, as for my life. Such ideas of the difference between **gentle** and **simple,** were, I believe, universal among all of my rank."

John Wesley's journal describes Robert Williams as simple. It describes his social rank not his personal gifts and intelligence. RW was an engaging and compelling preacher.

****

The first Methodist sermon preached in Virginia was unannounced street preaching. Mounting the court house steps in Norfolk, Robert Williams began to sing. His voice and Irish cadence were attractive. So was his appearance. He stood tall and strong, had a ruddy complexion and a well clothed (cloak and top hat) frame. With all the boldness of the experienced Irish street vender that he was, he sang the Charles Wesley hymn.

> Come, sinners, to the gospel feast,
> Let every soul be Jesus guest.
> Ye need not one be left behind,
> God hath bid all human kind.
> My message as from God receive;
> Ye all may come to Christ and live.
> O let his love your hearts constrain,
> Nor suffer him to die in vain.

Williams preaching was plain and direct. Everyone could understand the sermon. His words rang out across the crowd, "Fear, yes! Fear the fires of Hell"

"And flee, yes flee the wiles of the devil."

He spoke the words 'hell' and 'devil' so often and so bluntly with his Irish brogue that some folks thought he was swearing. Others wondered if he was sane. He certainly did not come across as gentle. Yet when they heard his message and observed his earnest compassion for each of them they were moved to hear him again.

He went to his knees, lifted his arms toward heaven and prayed for the city of Norfolk. With his final "Amen" there came responding "Amens."

"I will be staying among you for a while. I will preach at his same place tomorrow at 10:00 o'clock.' Robert Williams said. "Is there by chance a kind soul here today that will provide lodging for a servant of the Word of God?" That request was met with cold silence. Many looked away. Most turned away. Then a distinguished looking woman accompanied by a servant stepped forward. "You may stay in my guest cottage. I will have Betty prepare your lodging."

His benefactor was the wife of a sea captain. She had been converted by the preaching of George Whitfield, and was acquainted with Wesley's tracts and some of his sermons.

After dinner, Robert Williams read a Psalm and prayed for this household. He especially prayed for the Captain who was at sea. He asked God's Spirit to reach out across the waves and touch the heart of this good man. He prayed that he too would receive the gift of faith.

Weeks later when the Captain had reached harbor he told his lady about a strange spiritual experience he had in his cabin on the ship. "Suddenly, I was gripped by a mysterious presence. It was warm and kind. An assurance and confidence surrounded me. I was moved to pray. Before my prayer ended I was praising the Lord Jesus Christ. I received a mighty peace right then and there."

When the captain's wife asked about the day and time of this happening, she learned that it was at the very hour that Robert Williams had prayed for him and the household.

Robert Williams was remembered, wherever he went, as one who had "soul care." His prayers were often spoken through tears and always with sincerity. Robert Williams was a praying preacher, an obedient servant of the word, a compassionate curate and a great man of God.

Yeargain's Chapel

Samuel Yearrgain's land in the Roanoke Valley was on the north side of the river. Pigeon Roost Creek ran along one side. The 1100 acres stretched all the way down to the river. All of it lay in Bute County North Carolina. (*later it became Warren County*). Samuel Yeargain, an Irish farmer from County Limerick, came to the colonies in 1759. This was fertile bottom land and Yeargain cared for it diligently. He always left a place better than he found it.

The timber on the land made possible extra ordinary log buildings. He built a log house not a log cabin. The out buildings were useful and efficient. The kitchen, dairy, blacksmith shop, root cellar, and stable were all substantial. The spring house had a brook of cool spring water running through the middle of it. It was a very special place. When his wife went to get butter, milk or vegetables kept cool in the brook, she often lingered and quieted herself. "He leads me beside still waters," she would say.

Not far from the spring house was a secluded plum thicket where Elizabeth Yeargain prayed. The Yeargain's were faithful followers of the Methodist Way. One day, late in the morning, she went there to pray. Suddenly the whole area around her was ablaze with light. It was the brightest light that she had ever seen. It was dazzling white and brighter than the sun. It circled her all around. Elizabeth was terrified and fell to her knees in prayer.

At first she did not tell anyone about the light. She wondered if she should tell Samuel, or just keep it to herself.

That evening, just before they were going to blow out the lamp, she said, "Samuel. The strangest thing happened today while I was praying in the woods. A bright white light came all around me. Even though the place was shaded by trees, the light came. It was brighter than anything I have ever seen. What do you think it was?"

Samuel Yeargain had spent many years with the scriptures. He read them every day and meditated on them every night. In class meeting they had talked and studied about times when "the light shone all around" It was associated with a manifestation of God. In some places the scriptures teach that no one can see God and live.

Now he thought long and hard about this bright light that his lady had seen in her praying place. Elizabeth," he said gently, "it may have been the glory—the shekinah glory—the Glory of God"

"What does it mean?" the devout woman asked.

"Perhaps it means you will die soon," answered Yeargain. "Are you willing?"

"Yes I am willing" she said. "But I hope it will not be a long illness that takes me. I don't want the family to have to attend me through a long weakness. And I pray that I may be spared a painful death."

Together they talked about the bright shining light on the mount of transfiguration and about the light that blinded Saul of Tarsus on the road to Damascus. After the disciple Peter fell down before the light on the mountain, he wanted to build three tabernacles. That idea appealed to Samuel Yeargain.

Within a few short weeks, another log building stood on the plantation of Samuel and Elizabeth. It was a chapel— Yeargain's Chapel; a cornerstone for Christian faith on the Roanoke.

Robert Williams came to Samuel Yeargain's place in 1772 and preached in the newly constructed chapel. He organized a class and Yeargain's Chapel became a regular meeting place on the Brunswick Circuit.

One evening, Samuel told the story of the bright shining light that Elizabeth had seen. He told Robert Williams that he thought it meant that his wife would die soon

"That's not the only thing that is associated with shekinah glory," said RW. "When the young Isaiah saw the "Glory of God" in the temple, he also heard his call." *"Whom shall I send and who will go for me?"* He answered, "Here am I. Send me."

To experience the glory of God is a fearful thing. You can't stay the way you are.

Yeargain's Chapel became the cradle of Methodism in the south.

The Maryland Circuit

An Irish farmer and lay preacher came to America in 1760. His name, Robert Strawbridge, would find a place in Methodist History. He started the first class meeting and built the first Methodist chapel. He was a good farmer, but he was a great preacher. Wherever he preached people flocked to hear him. Many were convicted of their need for God's grace and convinced of Christ's redeeming power.

Landing in Philadelphia he followed a new road toward the lands that had been overrun by Indians in 1755. Now the French and Indian war was ending and the British had regained the territory. Land was available. Settlers were welcomed.

When Strawbridge and his wife Elizabeth came to Sam's Creek in Frederick County, they looked for a place to stay. John England owned a log home close to Windsor. It was for rent. Strawbridge lived in that home and farmed that land as a tenant for more than a dozen years. He bought it for fifty pounds in March of 1773. It was not only home for the Irish farmer and his family, it was also the gathering place for Irish lay preachers from the Palatines. One was Robert Williams. The other was the doctor, lay preacher, John King.

These three circuit riders became a band of brothers who spread Biblical holiness across Maryland. They rode together to the first general conference in America when it met in Philadelphia in 1773.

Reports were given and numbers showed that there were more new Methodist believers in the Maryland settlements than anywhere else in the colonies. Christian joy and good fellowship graced the meeting. There were also some confronting challenges.

Thomas Rankin had been given authority by John Wesley to establish order within the societies. "My dear brothers, let me put this question to you," said Rankin, "Shall we submit ourselves to the teachings and guidelines of John Wesley?"

Robert Strawbridge knew what was at stake in that question. Wesley did not allow lay preachers to administer the sacraments of baptism and communion. "RW," Strawbridge whispered, "This is going to be hard for me. I have already baptized new converts. I have served the sacrament. There was not an ordained priest within a hundred miles." The conference voted to honor Wesley's rules. Robert Strawbridge abstained from voting.

Later in the conference the presiding Rankin asked, "Shall we forbid the printing of any of John Wesley's writings by members of the societies?" Now Robert Williams leaned over to Strawbridge and said, "This is going to be hard for me. My saddlebags and my chests are filled with Wesley's writings that I have already printed. They are very much welcomed in the classes." RW was forthright as he reported his printing enterprise, and with some avail. The question was answered. "There shall be no more printing of Wesley's writings without his permission, but Robert Williams may continue to distribute what he has already printed."

John King, the third of this band of Irish brothers was a doctor. It took more than a little confidence and boldness to practice medicine in the 1760's. Remedies and interventions were always severe and not very gentle. King was blessed with more than his share of "holy boldness." He could cut close to the nerve. His style in preaching was also mighty bold. After hearing his sermon at the conference, Asbury commented, "It was long enough and loud enough." John

Wesley had once warned John King not to shout and scream in his preaching.

Francis Asbury had raised another concern at the conference. Some preachers wanted to stay in the cities. His philosophy as a traveling preacher was to ride, ride, ride.

Robert Strawbridge had enough reasons to stay on the farm rather than travel, but he was committed to open air preaching and to riding circuits. "There are folks in the cabins, sinners on the roads, settlers in the countryside, whom we can never reach unless we go after them where they are," said Strawbridge.

He continued, "No hunter would just sit in the house and wait for a turkey to come and be shot at. Fishermen don't throw their nets inside the boat and hope to catch fish. You're a street trader, brother Williams. You go to the markets; Peddlers follow their customers. They go out after business if it does not come to them; and so must we."

Some of our ordained brethren are preaching on and on to empty pews in empty churches. They could be bringing the gospel to hundreds of folks by quitting the church walls for a while. In one of the Lord's parables there is a command. 'Go out into the highways and bring them in!' Robert Strawbridge was forever a farmer, but he was always preaching.

On the way back to the Strawbridge's home they stopped at the John Evan's class meeting. They shared a good report of the conference and then asked Robert Williams to speak with them about matters of faith, before evening prayers. He talked about obedience, about subjecting yourself to a spiritual guide and to the scriptures. "In matters of faith," Robert Williams observed, "The next step is always obedience."

Robert Williams began to sing a Charles Wesley hymn. His brothers joined in.

I want a principle within
Of *jealous, godly fear, [*watchful]
A sensibility of sin,
A pain to feel it near.
I want the first approach to feel
Of pride or *fond desire, [*wrong]
To catch the wand'ring of my will,
And quench the kindling fire.
From Thee that I no more may part,
No more Thy goodness grieve,
The filial awe, the fleshly heart,
The tender conscience, give.
Quick as the apple of an eye,
O God, my conscience make;
Awake my soul when sin is nigh,
And keep it still awake.
Almighty God of truth and love,
To me Thy pow'r impart;
The mountain from my soul remove,
The hardness from my heart.
Oh, may the least omission pain
My reawakened soul,
And drive me to that blood again,
Which makes the wounded whole.

How does one take the measure of right and wrong; of faith and practice? To whom and to what may we offer ourselves for correction?

John Wesley offers the quadrilateral.
1. Is it faithful to scripture?
2. Is it faithful to reason?
3. Is it faithful to tradition?
4. Is it faithful to experience?

Settlers in the Valley

*St. Tammany was the name given
the new trading community around Blanton's Ferry*

A Place on the Roanoke

Patrick Goode applied for and was given a grant of 1500 acres of fertile bottom land along the Roanoke River near Blanton's ferry. It was on the condition he would settle on the land and bring two additional families with him. He persuaded two brothers, Patrick and Thomas King, to leave Ireland and come to America. He paid fifteen pounds each for their passage to the new world. In return they contracted to work for twelve months as indentured servants. Then each of them would be leased a hundred acres at modest rent. But first they must help clear and improve the settlement (*In Limerick they had only an eight acre lease that was farmed on shares*).

Patrick Goode intended to establish a plantation and build a fine house for himself, his wife and two small children. He had five slaves. He also owned two yoke of oxen, three horses, a carriage, a wagon, three cows and a flock of sheep. It was an impressive caravan that left the main road and turned south along a blazed trail leading to the new holdings.

A drover was assigned responsibility for the livestock that began to feast on the lush grass of the river bottoms. The rest of the party pitched an Indian tepee and then built a sturdy corral out of long pine poles. Before sunset on the third day, the walls of a cabin were in place. Patrick Goode called it "a pen" and now had his first defense against encroachment. That satisfied him. He knew what was his and was more than glad to defend it.

Even before the outside fences were finished he had organized his little company and two neighbors as the nucleus of a local militia. "Captain" Goode, as he now called himself, was taking charge.

This Irishman was "indefatigable." That was a favorite way of describing the unrelenting purpose of settlers, workers and traders on the frontiers of the colonies. It meant that Goode was a stubborn worker. There wasn't any quit in him. That's what also made him a grand "resister." His whole countenance showed it. Narrow set eyes, square jaw, jutted out chin and an unsmiling mouth all came together to say, "I won't back down!" Perpetual resistance had been his style from childhood. At age ten he had been flogged in the town square. Encouraged by the revolutionary spirit of the times, he had stood before the picture of King George and repeatedly shot him in the face with his sling shot. Captain

Goode was always on the lookout for any encroachment that he could resist.

The settlement and trading places around Blanton's ferry were given the name St. Tammany Landing. Chief Tammany befriended William Penn and responded to overtures of peace and friendship with the promise, "We will live side by side in peace and helpfulness, but I will defend what is mine." The illiterate chief made his sign on the deed: *a coiled snake*.

That philosophy suited colonists like Benjamin Franklin and Thomas Jefferson. They made it the philosophy of a secret society that encouraged resistance to King George. It was called St Tammany's Society. St. Tammany was the name given the new trading community around Blanton's ferry landing. This place was a good fit for Captain Goode. His style was resistance.

Michael Goode was not very happy when his wife became a Methodist. That had changed her boisterous partying ways. He liked a feisty woman, and now she was much too agreeable to suit the Captain. Try as he would, he could not raise any conflict with her; could not dissuade her desire to be a gentle woman. So, he decided to confront the Methodist circuit riders who had messed up his wife. Once on a trail in Maryland, he met a circuit rider, caught the bridle of the preacher's horse and challenged him to get down and fight. But the preacher was also a noncombatant.

Now here around Blanton's ferry and the Roanoke River plantations, horse racing, cock fighting, card playing and dancing were in vogue. Methodist circuit riders were met with plenty of resistance without any help needed from Captain Goode. So he began to satisfy his need to resist, protect and defend, by taking up the cause of the Methodists. He wasn't a confessing Methodist, but he considered himself their friend and took their side in every argument. He hoped it would be considered goodness on judgment day. That change in the captain greatly pleased his lady.

They were well settled, and had been for over a year. Then one day yard dogs heard something coming and stirred from their sleep. They began to bark. Ms. Mary, the long time kitchen slave looked up to see what had roused them. A man on horseback was coming toward the cabin; not fast, just steady. Ignoring the dogs he called out to the woman, "Hello, Hello." When he reached the yard gate he stopped, held up a flat, open hand to quiet the dogs and called out loudly, "Hello to the main house!" Captain Goode came out onto the porch, stood there fixed and tall for a moment, and then lifted his hand with a friendly greeting. He moved to the gate, hushed the still barking dogs, and took the measure of this horseman he'd never seen before in these parts.

He was well mounted on a magnificent horse. The saddlebags were packed for traveling. A beaver top hat and flowing cloak framed the stalwart body and ruddy face of a man's man. Every thing about him suggested that he was going to be the one in charge.

Robert Williams, Irish street preacher and colonial circuit rider, knew how to come up to a house. He knew how to come into a room. Some people try to slip in unnoticed. Others have an edge to them. Their approach makes everyone and everything uneasy. This circuit rider knew how to come up to your house. From the first moment you were glad to have him there and expected the visit to be significant.

"Are you a preacher?" Asked Captain Goode.

"Indeed I am; and a Methodist!"

"Well step down then so that we can meet on the level. I've never taken up religion. My lady has. In fact she has had Methodist beginnings."

A boy about 10 years old had come to his father's side. "Billy, take the man's horse to the stable. Get him some corn and a fork full of that grass hay. Then hurry back up to the house. We've got a mighty interesting visitor here today."

Robert Williams took his saddle bags from in back of the saddle. He threw them over his shoulder as the two men started for the house.

"Thank you for the warm welcome." Williams said. I'll be needing a place to stay tonight, Shall I expect to stay over a bit?".

"I am not going to answer that question," said Goode. Let's go up to the house and meet my good wife , Winnifried. We'll let her decide."

Petersburg Society

Devereux Jarratt

I was in my 31ˢᵗ year, when I took upon me the pastoral charge of some thousands of souls, in the county of Dinwiddie, and parish of Bath. An awful charge! Who is sufficient for these things?

Devereux Jarratt (1733-1801) was the son of a common (not wealthy) white family in Virginia (his father was a carpenter). He was very young when his father died and therefore went to live with his older brother. There was little or no interest in religion on this plantation. He exercised race horses and supervised fowl for cock fighting.

He did not attend college, but with the gift of exceptional memory he gained academic excellence. As a young man he was employed as the a tutor to the sons of John Cannon, an evangelical Presbyterian and wealthy land owner. He felt the first stirring of religious belief while listening to Cannon's wife read pious tracts to her children.

Jarratt began to meet with local Presbyterian ministers engaged in the work of religious revival. He wanted to become an Anglican priest. After completing the necessary reading, he went to London to be examined by the Church. He was approved and ordained by the Bishop of London. On his return to America in 1762 he was installed as rector of Bath Parish.

Jarratt reached his widest fame as a leader of the Great Awakening in Virginia during the 1760s and 1770s. He participated in this revivalist movement as an Anglican and Episcopalian . Devereux Jarratt's ministry was shaped by his experience of "new birth" and his commitment to biblical holiness. He preached on long circuits from Petersburg into North Carolina.

Robert Williams was the first Methodist preacher to visit Father Jarratt. It was in 1772. On that first visit he stayed for a week. Devereux Jarratt liked him. Hew wrote to his friend, John Coleman saying, "Mr. Robert Williams, is a plain, unpretentious, pious man. He came to my house, in the year 1772, and stayed near a week. He preached several sermons in the parish, most, or all of which I heard. I liked his preaching."

"Mr. Williams also furnished me with some of their books, and I became acquainted with the minutes of several of their conferences. By these means I was let into their general plan, and the view that "He that left the [Anglican] church, left the Methodists?' I put a strong mark on these words. I felt much attachment to Mr. Williams,"

As an ordained Anglican priest, Father Jarratt celebrated the sacrament of Holy Communion regularly. Robert Williams, like all of John Wesley's lay preachers, looked to the parish ministers of the Anglican church for baptism and holy communion.The circuit riders travelled to "call sinners to repentance" and to do all they could for "the spiritual improvement of the societies." The Methodist lay preachers wanted to build up and not to divide the church.

Robert Williams did not schedule any preaching services at a time when he was near a church that had a service scheduled for the same time. But often he stood outside the church, usually on a grave stone in the cemetery, and exhorted the people as they left the service. They stayed to listen. Many souls were awakened.

"Father Jarratt," RW began, "It is a joyful and wondrous thing to eat the bread and drink the cup and so remember our dear dying Friend. It grieves me that some of the baptized don't care at all. There were only eight people at the altar today and all of them were old."

(*The sacrament of the supper had been so little regarded, in Virginia, by what were called Church people that, generally speaking, none went to the table at all.*)

"I was like them, Robert. And so were my brothers. But as soon as my eyes were opened to see the necessity of a Savior, I wanted to remember the cross, and as you say it, 'our dying Friend."

The Petersburg Society was formed where these two men taught and preached. Their sermons were shaped by purity and humility. Father Jarratt added a traveling, itinerant ministry to his regular parish duties. Williams joined with him and they preached tirelessly across the countryside of southern Virginia and into North Carolina.

The number of persons attending the services of Holy Communion also increased dramatically. Jarratt said, "The number was, at least, nine hundred or one thousand."

Source: *The Life of the Reverend Devereux Jarratt . . . Written by Himself, . . .* (Baltimore, 1806), 14, 43-44, 83-86.

Merrymount Plantation

Headed for a Warm Stable

Colonel Davis was mighty proud of his plantation on the south side of the Roanoke River. Tobacco was the cash crop and the dock on the river made it convenient to get the crop to market.

The plantation was self sufficient. The vegetable garden and herb garden were close by the kitchen. There was a smoke house, a spring house where the butter and cream from the dairy house were kept. There was a weaver's house, a blacksmith house, a store house, a hog house, cattle shed and a very fine stable for the horses. On the outside edges of the plantation were the servant's cabins.

Colonel Davis was known for his fine horses, as was all of Mecklenburg County. A round race track at Boydton Virginia was the place where the big race events were schedule each spring. Match races on a straight track were frequently held on the plantations. Horse racing, cock fighting, and barn dancing were all social occasions. The Methodist circuit rider, Robert Williams preached against all of them.

That however did not prevent the employment of his fine stallion, Traveler, in the siring of blooded horses. Colonel Davis' had a foal born in 1774 that he named Polly Williams.

Robert Williams had been preaching on the Brunswick Circuit and crossed the Roanoke on the flat boat at Tammany's landing. It was early in March 1773 and he was on his way to the Jerusalem class meeting scheduled at Ebenezer Coleman's plantation. A late snow storm had blown in. RW was looking for the first shelter he could find. A short way up from the river he came to Merrymount. Colonel Davis welcomed him.

Next morning they were in the stable together and Davis was admiring the gray stallion. "That's a mighty fine horse you've got," Mr. Williams. "He shows excellent breeding."

RW told him of the time he found him abandoned in a stable on Staten Island. After he had gentled the angry stallion he had traced his pedigree. It was excellent. Now the horse had carried him all through the colonies.

"He has been ridden a long way this winter hasn't he?" observed the Colonel. "I am pleased that I could give him a warm rest and a good breakfast in my stable."

If the truth were told, it is likely that the horse racing, Colonel Davis, would rather host the circuit rider's horse than the circuit rider. The magnificent horses on the Merrymount were better cared for than most persons.

Colonel Davis seldom missed an opportunity to gather more and improve what he had. "Would you like to trade or sell your stallion? Tell me you price."

"No. I will never sell my saddle, and I will never sell this horse. He's the legs beneath me. He's my eyes and ears in the dark woods. He's my safety through the waters. He's even my praying place. He's not for sale at any price."

Robert Williams cast an affectionate eye toward his fine stallion, and was warmed to see the horse so contented in this excellent stable. He wished that he could stay for a while; at least until the grass was growing again.

Davis must have read his mind. "Mr. Williams, if you will not sell me your stallion, would you consider leasing him to me for sixty days? I would like for him to get friendly with some of my mares. I'll pay you well for his services and provide you with a horse and chaise for your travels."

The devout traveling preacher never made a decision with out at first taking the measure of it by the teachings of scripture. This guideline came to him; Genesis 1:28 "Be fruitful and increase. Fill the earth and subdue it." The Methodist preacher, Robert Williams would long be remembered in horse racing circles along the Roanoke.

A foal was born in early 1774. Her sire was Traveler. Colonel Davis named her Polly Williams. She grew into a splendid horse with extra ordinary speed and grace. Tradition tells s that she was never beaten in a match race. Colonel Davis wagered large sums on every one of them. He came away a winner.

Robert Williams didn't ever talk about that. He didn't like to hear about it. He still preached against horse racing and gambling, cockfighting and dancing. But RW was secretly proud of the offspring of his stallion, Traveler.

Colonel Davis liked the circuit rider. He never liked him as much as he liked his horse, but he liked him. In fact whenever there was a "dinner on the grounds" along the river, Davis and his people would be there. They even stayed for the singing and the preaching.

. .

Dinner on the Grounds

Word spread all along the south side of the Roanoke that there was going to be a great gathering and dinner on the grounds in the apple yard at Maratuc.

Bobby and Janie Kilpatrick built their home overlooking the Roanoke River where it was joined by Smith Creek. They named their place Maratuc, the Indian name for the Roanoke. On the high side of their land there was a lovely pond. Trees had been cleared and an apple orchard planted. The apple trees were a grand attraction for deer. That's why fresh venison was always on hand. The guest house on the edge of the pond was a favorite haven for Robert Williams. He often preached at the edge of the orchard.

Dinner on the grounds always drew a crowd. There would be Methodist singing and testifying. Now word spread that Robert Williams was going to preach at Maratuc on a Sunday just two weeks away All of the God fearing folks in the neighborhood made plans to be there. Even the non religious neighbors expected to join in the feasting. It promised to be a great day on the Roanoke.

Settlers got up early to finish their chores. Women folk prepared great baskets of food. Horses were hitched to buggies. Oxen were yoked to the wagons. The roads and trails, usually quiet, were bustling with travelers.

The gathering was to begin at 10:00 AM with singing, praise and prayers, but at first light, Anne Rose and her son Robbie were already cooking a brunswick stew. Venison, rabbit and squirrel meat had boiled all night in a big iron pot. Now potatoes, onions, tomatoes, corn and butterbeans were added to the tender meat and broth. The fire was kept hot. The pot was almost boiling. Stirring never stopped. A brunswick stew required a good deal of labor, but it added so much to a meeting with it's fragrance and uniqueness, that someone always stepped up to serve stew.

Not far from the stew pot a group of men were sharing stories. At first they told about corn husking. Then they turned to some hunting and gathering tales. Chad Kilpatrick, Bobby and Janie's son, was very clever along the river and streams. He knew every tributary and every back water pond. He was also skilled with a bow and arrow. He told about the 400 pound black bear he killed with one well placed arrow. Only yesterday he had taken a wild turkey. It would be part of the feast today.

"Did you hear about Sir Richard Allen's goose hunting adventure?" Bobby Kilpatrick asked. "If Robert Williams hadn't come along at just the right time he likely would have died in the cold."

In November and December great flights of Canadian geese filled the skies along the Roanoke. Reedy Marsh was a favorite resting place for them. That was the place to go if you wanted a Christmas goose.

Usually one of Sir Richard's slaves would do the goose hunting, but one December day he chose to do it himself. Hunting was good sport for the gentry. From the Indians he had learned how to make a "root head decoy." Feathers would be bound to a frame with honeysuckle vines. Then a tree root, shaped like the neck and head of a goose, would be attached. Four or five decoys would attract a flock of geese.

Sir Richard was well concealed in his blind in the reeds along the edge of the water. His muzzle loader was loaded and primed. He had only one shot. It needed to be well planned and well placed. More than twenty geese circled and then landed in front of his hiding place. The hunter picked out a fine gander, steadied the musket and fired. Black smoke, flapping wings and noisy honking filled the air. When the smoke cleared he could see that the gander was the only goose left. It had a broken wing. Sir Richard climbed into his canoe and went to retrieve it.

He grabbed the goose by the neck, and a battle began. A goose with a broken wing can't fly, but it can give you an awful "wing beating.' As it was trying to pull away, it got Sir Richard out over the edge of his craft. The canoe began tipping but Sir Richard held on. He held on and held on until over it went. Sir Richard Allen was up to his neck in freezing water.

With his captured goose in hand he started back to his blind. The water was too deep and with boots on he couldn't swim. He tried to get back in the canoe, but try as he might he couldn't do it. He waded in shallower water toward the other shore. Exhausted and freezing he threw himself and the goose up on the bank, staggered to his feet and began to walk. He got as far as the road. That's where Robert Williams found him, almost frozen to death.

RW loaded him up in his buggy, took him to the nearest cabin, arranged to get him dry and warm, and went back for his goose and his gun. Someone could get the canoe later.

It was at the Christmas roast goose dinner that Sir Richard Allen testified, "Robert Williams has helped save many souls. Let me tell you how he saved my life."

The crowd had gathered for the" dinner on the grounds" feast. After the morning singing the long tables were covered with food from the baskets. Four meal time prayers were said. First the youngest class leader prayed; second a faithful woman; third the oldest class leader; finally the circuit rider, Robert Williams. It occasioned another of his Irish poems:

> May you have food and raiment,
> A soft pillow for your head,
> May you be forty years in heaven
> Before the devil knows you're dead.

An awakening was spreading through out the Roanoke Valley. Societies formed and classes were organized in the homes. Hebron, Macon, Warrenton, Jerusalem, Zion, and Palmer Springs were places where Methodist class meetings would grow into Methodist churches. Methodism was gaining ground on the south side of the Roanoke River.

Ebenezer Coleman's

At Coleman's Robert Williams organized the class
that became Jerusalem UMC

Arriving at Tammany's ferry, Robert Williams asked the
slave who was poling the flat boat across the water,
"Does any one in these parts read the Bible and pray?"
"Ebenezer Coleman and his lady do," the boatman answered."
"Does he live along the ferry road?" asked the circuit rider.

"Yes he does! About two miles further on south. He's
a good man He's a Methodist. He'll likely take you in."
A woman with a dairy cow was waiting at the ferry. They
loaded her cow first; then the preacher and his horse.
Methodist preaching was headed toward the big oak tree
on the plantation of Ebenezer Coleman. Seeds planted there
would become Jerusalem United Methodist Church.

There were four slave families that lived in the cabins of
the Coleman plantation. The ferry road ran past them. Eliza,

a strong and able woman, lived in the first cabin. She was the trusted kitchen servant in the big house. The children ran to tell her that a man riding a horse and reading a book was coming up the road. She went out to greet him.

Robert Williams, reigned in his horse, stepped down and walked over to the rail fence. "Hello gentlewoman," he said. "I've been told that your people are God fearing; that they read the Bible and pray. Is that true?"

"Oh, yes sir it is. And we are all blessed because of it. Are you the Methodist circuit riding preacher we've heard tell about?" "I am Robert Williams and I have come to preach the gospel. Will you please send word to the main house that I am here?"

"Preaching man, I already know that you're good and welcome. Come through that gate yonder. I'll just take you right up to the big house." said Eliza

The whole plantation buzzed with excitement. Ebenezer Coleman knew that the preacher was in the lane even before he saw him. His greeting was, "How good it is that you have come. We have been asking God to send us someone to encourage us and teach us in the faith. How good it is to look out the door of my house and see a Methodist preacher. You must stay with us for a while. We'll invite neighbors to come, even tonight, to hear you preach." The crowd that gathered was gay and noisy, but RW gained attention. He sang a hymn; he prayed, he preached and he prayed again. His text was, "Behold the Lamb of God who takes away sin."

"Let me tell you about your dear dying friend. He shed his blood to save you from the wrath of God," he began. He preached with warmth and holy boldness. The believers in the room responded with affirmation and praise.

The next morning Captain Coleman took RW out to the spot he intended to clear for a preaching place. A giant oak tree shaded the area. Its spreading branches would echo the preacher's songs and sermons. William's spirit was refreshed as he prayed on this holy ground. "Our Lord would have liked this quiet place," he said, commenting on how Jesus often withdrew to a quiet place to pray.

"Mr. Williams," began Coleman, "No doubt you noticed how loud and lively the crowd was last evening. It's always that way when Methodists gather. Maybe it's not as quiet as some would like it to be. There is a lot of happiness and a lot of talking."

"A Presbyterian preacher came to preach at the meeting house on the old trading route. There was a lot of happy talk going on there. The preacher didn't approve. He told us that if we had to talk we should whisper; just whisper a prayer. Zeke Miller and I were having a good talk so we kept on visiting. After services I was moved to explain to the preacher about our talking in church."

Zeke Miller is a good man, but he's poor and has five children to feed. He has only one milk cow, and that cow got tangled in brush. She cut her udder real bad. Dried her up; .she wouldn't milk. When I sat down on the plank behind Zeke, we started talking about his problem. I asked him, "What are you going to do for milk for the children?"

"I don't know, I just don't know," said Miller. "Well, Zeke," I said, "I have five cows that are giving milk right now. It's more than we need around our place. Tomorrow morning, we'll bring one of our cows down to you. Keep her until your young cow freshens."

"I told that Presbyterian prayer whispering preacher what we were talking about. And I told him, that after we had shared the problem and got milk for the family, both Zeke Miller and I were more ready to praise God."

"That's a great story," said Robert Williams. "There are times for quiet and there are times for talk. I like Methodist happiness. I like the singing, and I like Methodist enthusiasm even a bit of shouting."

A Place to Be

The Circuit Rider's Lady

There were more than six hundred new converts in the meetings that made up the Brunswick Circuit. They were gathered into classes. Class leaders needed Bibles, devotional materials, and study books. Robert Williams had been providing some of these wherever he went, but now there was an apparent need for a printing and publishing concern among the Methodists.

When in Williamsburg he went to the printing shop where the Virginia Gazette was published. It was more than a news paper office. The shop served as a stationer's, a post office, an advertising agency, an office supply shop, a newsstand, and a bookbindery. Magazines and books, maps and almanacs, and even sealing wax were sold there. The press printed broadsides and business forms, laws and proclamations, tracts and blank record books.

"I can do that," the industrious and untiring Robert Williams said. "I cannot publish a news paper or print government documents without being licensed as a master printer, but I can set type and my used printing press can be well employed for the Lord. There's a good market for the services of a print shop in Norfolk."

He was right in his judgment and successful in his plan. The Irish peddler, Wesleyan preacher, colonial circuit rider had become a business man in Norfolk, Virginia."

Robert Williams had a favorite preaching place near Suffolk. George Washington had a compelling interest in the Dismal Swamp. He wanted to drain portions of it and use the fertile land for planting. His expeditions into the swamp took him through Suffolk. He stayed there often. The Dismal Swamp was not an attraction for RW. Rather it was the Methodist class meeting in Judith Delaney's home.

Mrs. Delaney was two times a widow. When she was only seventeen, Judith Owens married a sailor. He was first mate on a square rigger and his journeys were very profitable. He provided well for his young bride. They had been married for three years when he was lost at sea. There were no children.

The young widow grew strong and gentle through her grief. She was awakened by the preaching of George Whitfield and became a faithful member of the Burroughs Anglican Church in Norfolk. That is where she met and married her second husband. Mr. Delaney was a well established merchant who was twenty years older than Judith. Their new residence was near Suffolk on the road to Norfolk. It had a well built two story home along with two servant's cottages and a guest house.

Mrs. Judith Delaney was thirty one years old when she became a widow for the second time. Still there were no children. She found faith, hope and charity to be the virtues that she could trust. "Does anything last forever?" she asked herself. "Yes, faith hope and love abide." (1 Corinthians 13)

She heard Robert Williams preach first in Norfolk, and then in Portsmouth in Isaac Luke's home. After his preaching in Suffolk, she was one of those who helped establish the class meeting. Soon she was chosen to be the leader. The class grew to number more that thirty men and women. When ever Robert Williams preached anywhere in the area, they were there.

The class became interested in printed materials — Bibles and devotional materials. They had learned of John Wesley's recommended devotional lists. One was the writing of Thomas A' Kempis. He recommended "The Imitation of Christ" as a guideline for holy living. "Will you print us a tract that includes some of those teachings?" Judith Delaney asked RW. Together they made some selections.

As they paged through Robert Williams' copy of "The Imitation of Christ" they came to a chapter addressing familiarity. Thomas A'Kempis counseled, *"Be not familiar with any woman,"* they quickly passed over that section without any comment at all.

The next chapter, "Of Obedience and Subjection," was chosen as copy for the tract. It reads, *"It is verily a good thing to live in obedience, to be under authority, and not to be at your own disposal."* Robert Williams was a kind and sensitive man. He was strong enough to gentle and wise enough to abide error. He was painfully honest and very out spoken, but never authoritarian. He commented on the teaching. "Perhaps the most important question one can be asked in the class meetings is this, "To whom or to what teaching will you offer yourself for correction?"

In Suffolk a special friendship was growing. The guest house at Judith Delaney's was the place RW stayed when he was in the area. Every one needs a place to be. Robert Williams, like his Lord could say, "Foxes have holes. Birds of the air have their nests. But I have no place to lay my head." How good it would be to have a place to call home.

Robert William's strength and ability, his devotion and virtue, his warmth and charm, and his gifts and graces as a preacher were legend wherever he went. Many people admired him, welcomed him and loved him as a friend. But he had no primary relationship, no significant other.

It would be fair to say that the widow Delaney made the first move. It was not assertive or predatory. It was respectful, honest and entirely proper. She invited him for dinner and told him plainly that he would be the only guest. One of her servants would be in the house and would help her serve the meal.

It was a candle light dinner. Fresh flowers graced the table. RW had been guest at many well appointed dinners in the plantation houses along the Roanoke. This was the first time that he would dine alone with a very attractive woman.

There was such integrity in their conversation, such purity and respect in their hearts, such genuine regard for each other, that from the out set neither was uncomfortable. This was the kind of meeting that Robert Williams and Judith Delaney hoped would happen again.

Seated together in the porch swing, Ms. Judith spoke first. "RW." That's what she called him now, "What is the most wonderful teaching in the Holy Bible?" He didn't hesitate for a moment. He simply began to sing. "Jesus loves me this I know, for the Bible tells me so. Little ones to him belong. I am weak, but he is strong." The lady began to sing with him. Their voices joined—even blended, "Yes Jesus loves me. Yes Jesus loves me. Yes Jesus loves me. The Bible tells me so."

She said that she wanted to walk him back to the guest house. On the way he took her hand. At the door he kissed it. Three days later he asked for that hand in marriage. She said yes and when he returned from preaching throughout the circuit they were married by the Anglican priest at the Burroughs in Norfolk.

Their home was not just a place to be. God blessed their union and their home became a place of comfort and joy. This was true not only for them, but for all who had the good fortune to visit their home. When visitors left, love was no longer a stranger to them. They witnessed it in the special bond of this man and this woman who had in Christ become one.

Robert Williams requested location at the conference of 1775. That meant he would no longer serve as one of the circuit riders of the Roanoke Valley. But he would always be a friend of the Methodist Way and a herald of the gospel.

His printing enterprises would pass on to John Dickens. They were the beginning of the great Methodist Book Concern. His supply of Bibles, sermons, tracts and religious study books began to strengthen and anchor Christian teaching in the homes of thousands of new converts.

The Suffolk Society and especially Ms. Judith's class meeting became noted for its prayer warriors.

The circuit riders who followed in the steps of Robert Williams found gracious hospitality in his home. The guest book recorded names that would be forever remembered in Methodist history: Asbury, PIlmoor, John King, Rankin, Shadford, Jesse Lee, Watters, Andrew Geargain, Gatch, and John Dickens. Bishop Asbury came to this home often.

I am bound for the Promised Land

On Jordan's stormy banks I stand
And cast a wishful eye
To Canaan's fair and happy land
Where my possessions lie
All o'er those wide extended plains
Shines one eternal day
There God, the Son forever reigns
And scatters night away.
No chilling wind nor poisonous breath
Can reach that healthful shore
Where sickness, sorrow, pain and death
Are felt and feared no more
When shall I see that happy place
And be forever blessed
When shall I see my Father's face
And in His bosom rest

W hen Bishop Asbury came to Norfolk in the fall of 1775 he went immediately to the home of Judith Delany Williams. Robert Williams had died.

There was extraordinary stress in the newspaper offices of the *Intelligencer in September '75.* The sons of liberty and the British had been contesting their opinions through every media available. The Norfolk paper was an aggravation to the Earl of Dunsmore, the Governor of Virginia.

To protect himself from revolutionary hatred he had moved his offices to a British ship anchored in the Norfolk harbor. On the fateful day when Robert Williams died, Dunsmore sent soldiers into the city to confiscate the press and shut down the news paper. There was nothing and no one to stop them.

Robert Williams was warned of their coming. He threw himself into frenzied labor gathering and boxing books, tracts and Bibles. He needed to save printed materials that were important to the Methodist Way. He hired a team and wagon and began to load the contents of the print shop. The driver, not wanting to get involved, just sat on the wagon seat. Robert Williams did it all. He packed and he carried, he lifted and loaded one heavy box after another. It was more one man should try to do.

Just before the British came down the street, he had rounded the corner and was headed for home. He was exhausted. Little did he know that he was closer to the Father's house right then, than to any place in this world. Before he reached home, there was a searing pain in his chest. Servants helped him inside, and his lady helped him to his bed. They sent for a doctor.

"Judith, please read to me," said Robert Williams. There is a copy of *"The Pilgrim's Progress"* near my big chair. I marked the place where I was reading last evening.

Judith Delaney Williams, sat down next to her dying husband and read from John Bunyan's vision of crossing the river. *"Now I further saw that betwixt them and the gate, was the River of Death. There was no bridge to go over, and the river was deep."*

"At sight thereof the pilgrims were much stunned, asking if there was no other way. Being told there was none, they addressed themselves to the water. Having entered it, Christian began to sink; but Hopeful cried, "Be of good cheer, my brother; I feel the bottom."

"Yes! Yes!" said Robert Williams. "Be of good cheer my darling; be of good cheer my friends; be of good cheer Christians everywhere. I feel the bottom and it is good."

His heart failed at age 42 He came to America when he was thirty seven years old. His ministry was brief, only six years. His birth date is uncertain, sometime in 1733. He died on September 25, 1775.

When Bishop Asbury arrived at the widow Williams' home she met him in the "withdrawing room." They wept together; prayed together; shared the Psalms and Gospels together; and then they remembered RW. They recalled his special strengths, so plain, so caring, so stubborn and unrelenting, so bold and direct, so compassionate and personal; so useful in the cause of Christ.

After planning the funeral service they walked together toward the guest house where RW used to stay before he married. Asbury noticed the apple tree under which circuit riders had often preached. The apples were ready to be picked and some had fallen. So had some leaves. He recalled the prophet Isaiah's words, "The grass withers, the flowers fade, but the word of God endures forever."

One of the class members recalled what Robert Williams once said to a grieving but confident gathering of Christian mourners, "As Easter people, we can give up our dead as easily as that tree gives up its leaves in autumn."

Judith Delaney Williams, breathed a silent prayer, "Please God, let something remain."

History Selections referencing the "Old Book"

⧫

79412

THE EARLY HISTORY

OF

AMERICAN METHODISM.

By Rev. J. B. WAKELEY.

About Robert Williams

ROBERT WILLIAMS was a local preacher from England, who came to this country in the early part of the year 1769. Mr. Wesley gave him a permit to preach in America under the direction of his missionaries. Mr. Williams arrived here before Richard Boardman and Joseph Pilmoor, and was employed in Wesley Chapel, preaching the Gospel. His Irish friend, the noble-hearted Ashton, generously paid his passage to this country. Mr. Williams was so poor he was unable to pay it himself. He not only preached in NewYork before the arrival of the regular missionaries, but was stationed there for a time in 1771. There has always been more or less of mystery connected with his name and history. What little we know of him makes us anxious to know more.

In the Minutes of the first conference, which was held in Philadelphia, June, 1773, is the following "*Robert Williams to sell the books he has already printed, but to print no more, unless under the above restrictions,"* which were these: " *None of the preachers in America to reprint any of Mr. Wesley's books without his authority (when it can be gotten) and the consent of their brethren."* This shows Mr. Williams was an enterprising man, and no doubt his little book enterprise was the germ of the gigantic Methodist Book Concern.

In the **"old book** " Mr. Williams' name is often mentioned, and we see what he did to promote Methodism in its infancy in this country. Whoever kept the book was so particular in recording everything that transpired, both great and small, that the reader is introduced to Mr. Williams, and permitted to behold him as he was in olden times; to listen to his preaching; then see him put on his " new hat," wrap his " new cloak " around him; to behold him in sickness, his physician feeling his pulse and looking at his tongue, then giving him medicine, and then sending in his bill to the trustees for payment. Again: he is seen in the. barber's shop; the barber lathers Mr. Williams' face, shaves him, then shampoos him, and combs and brushes his hair. The reader sees the mail arrive. Mr. Williams receives his letters, and the trustees pay the postage. He is introduced to Mr. Williams' horse, one of the very first on whose back an itinerant Methodist preacher ever rode in this country. He is seen in pasture in the midst of the clover, then with his master on his back, carrying him to his appointments. This is the pioneer horse, carrying the pioneer preacher to his pioneer work; the very first of a long line of noble and faithful animals who have carried the preachers around their circuits and districts. Methodist ministers have been proverbial for having good horses, many of which have been great favorites with their owners as well as with the people.

The following ___account of what was paid to Robert Williams, while preaching in John-street___, is taken from the " old book."

20th Sept. 1769. To cash paid Mr. Jarvis for a hat for Mr. Williams £ 2 5 0

22d Sept. " To cash for a book for Mr. Williams.. 009

9th Oct. " To cash paid Mr. Newton for three pair of stockings for

Mr. Williams and Mr. Embury Ill 9

To cash paid for a trunk for Mr.Williams 0 12 6

30th Oct. "To cash paid Mr. Williams to pay his expenses 116 0 To cash paid for a cloak for Mr.Robert Williams 8 0 6

March 1st, 1770. To cash paid for Mr. Williams's horse while at Doughlass's on Staten Island 316 8

March 20th, 1770. Cash paid Mr. Williams £5 8 0

March 20th, 1770 To ditto paid more for keeping his horse 012 0

10th April, 1770 To cash paid Dr. K Tesbit for attendance on Mr. Williams, &c 410 6

24th " " To flannel for Mr. Williams 030

llth June " To cash for a letter for Mr. Williams, from Dublin 0 2 8

26th July, " To John Beck for keeping Mr. Williams's horse 016 6

To cash paid Mr. Maloney for shaving preachers 2 5 6

Sept. " To postage on 2 letters, one for Mr.Pilmoor, one for Mr. Williams... 048 1771. April 15. To Mr. Newton, for Mr. Williams... 256 " Ang. 30.

To cash paid Caleb Hyatt, for Mr.Williams's horse-keeping 018 0

All this appears to us very singular, but we see how they did business in the cradle of American Methodism, before the writer or many of his readers were born. They paid for Mr. Williams's "hat," a "beaver hat," and for his "cloak;" also for his "trunk," " stockings," " book," " horse-keeping," " doctor's bill," "flannel," "postage," "barber's bill," and board. How differently preachers are provided for at the present time. There are two receipts in the "old book" in which Mr. Williams's name is mentioned ; one concerning his hat, which appears in our account of Mr. Jarvis, the other his doctor's receipt, which is appended. In the latter receipt it will be seen that Mr. Boardman was sick. Mr. Asbury says he " *found him weak in body when he arrived in New-York.*"

The first preachers who came from England were all sick, Williams, Boardman, Pilmoor; after that, Mr. Asbury. I have no doubt that they were going through the process of acclimating, a tribute which almost all have to pay who go to a strange country.

"Rec'd April 12, 1770, of Mr. William Lupton, four pounds, ten shillings, and sixpence, for medicine and attendance on Mr. Williams and Mr. Boardman.£4 10s. 6d.

Mr. Williams's acc't £4 2«. 0d.

Mr. Boardman's " Ss. 6d."

Physicians are more generous now; they seldom send in a bill to a clergyman for their professional services. We give the doctor's autograph with his receipt, as he was the first physician that doctored a Methodist minister in America.

I have before me a love-feast ticket which Hannah Dean, afterward the wife of Paul Hick, received from Robert Williams, in his own haud-writing. The following is a copy, with a fac-simile of Mr. Williams's autograph:

Psalm 147. 11. October 1. 1769. The Lord takth pleasure in them that fear him: in those that hope in his mercy. Hannah Dean. 75* *N. York*

There is a history in this solitary love-feast ticket. In the first place, its age invests it with no ordinary interest. It was one of the first given in this country, and that before the regular missionaries arrived. This was dated the 1st of October, 1769; Boardman and Pilmoor arrived the 24th of that month.Again: It was *witten,* not printed; the only written love-feast ticket in America that has descended to us from so early a period. This ticket shows there was method and order among the Methodists at that time. They were holding love-feasts, not with open, but closed doors, and had their love-feast tickets. It shows that Robert Williams had some charge of the society soon after his arrival, or he would not have issued love-feast tickets over his own signature. The modest Embury, never forward, but always retiring, no doubt rejoiced at the coming of Mr. Williams, and was glad to have the laboring oar rest with him.

To Philip Embury belongs the distinguished honor of preaching the first Methodist sermon, forming the first Methodist society, erecting the first Methodist house of worship, and preaching the first dedication sermon of the first Methodist house of worship consecrated to God in this new world. Honor to whom honor is due.

When Embury and his cousin, Barbara Heck, arrived in the colonies, they settled in New York. They appear to have associated themselves with the historic Trinity Church, that still stands as a landmark amid the rush and bustle of New York mercantile life. It was at Trinity that they received communion, and I have no doubt the old records would show that there there they went to be married and there they took their children to be baptized. We know that some of their associates were buried in the Trinity Church grounds.

Whether through falling from grace, or because Trinity satisfied their religious wants, they allowed six years to go by before resuming their own Methodistic services. In October, 1766, Philip Embury, the carpenter and former preacher, held the first service and preached the first Methodist sermon in his house on Barrick Street, now Park Place. The Palatines were again drawn together, and next year,1767, it was found necessary to rent a room near the Barracks, and a little later the Rigging Loft on Horse and Cart Street, now William Street, and here Embury and the old warrior, Captain Webb, who had fought at Quebec under Wolfe, preached to the Methodists with such fervour that the building of a chapel became necessary.

To build a chapel a lot was first required, so we find that on the 26th of March, 1768, Mary Barclay and three others, executors of the estate of Henry Barclay, conveyed lots 112 and 113 on John Street to Philip Embury, Wm. Lupton, Charles White, Richard Sause, Henry Newton, Paul Heck, Thos. Taylor and Thos. Webb. We recognize at least two of these trustees as our old friends from Ballingrane. Charles White and Richard Sause also were from Ireland, and Captain Thomas Webb is by some credited to the same country. Who were the Barclays ? Rev. Henry Barclay, D.D., was the second rector of Trinity Church (from 1746 to the date of his death, 1764), and Mary Barclay was his widow. The title deed was not signed until 1770, and some property adjoining was purchased in 1786 from the Dutch Reformed Church. The deeds do not bear the names of Embury and Heck, because they had left New York just before or at the time the final transfer of the property took place.

"A Society commonly called Methodists (under the direction of the Rev. Mr. John Wesley), whom it is evident God has been pleased to bless in their meetings in New York, thinking it would be more to the glory of God and the good of souls had they a more convenient place to meet in where the Gospel of Jeaus Christ might be preached without distinction of sects or parties ; and a Mr. Philip Embury is a member and helper in the Gospel, they humbly beg the assistance of Christian friends in order to enable them to build a small house for that purpose."

The building of the chapel began at once. Barbara Heck, we are told, supplied the plan ; a building with fireplace built like a large house, so that the rights of the Established Church would not be infringed upon. Philip Embury did much of the work ; he built the pulpit with his own hands.

*Paul Heck, £3 53.; Jacob Heck, £i ; Valentine Tetlor (or Detlor), £i ; David Embury, £2.*These are names on the list that suggest the Irish Palatines gave as much as they could. Philip Embury did not subscribe, perhaps because he was not able, but he gave time and labour, *The full list of subscriptions to the building fund may be found in Wakeley's " Lost Chapter of Methodism."*

On the 3Oth of October, 1768, Philip Embury preached the opening or dedicatory sermon. His text was Hosea 10:12. "Sow to yourselves in righteousness, reap in mercy, break up your fallow ground ; for it is time to seek the Lord, till lie come and rain righteousness upon you."

Philip Embury was for a time a trustee. He was also the first treasurer, and filled the office of preacher until **Rev. Robert Williams arrived from Ireland**. Mr. Wesley sent out Rev. Richard Boardman and Rev. Joseph Pilmoor in the fall of 1769. For some years this building on John Street was known as Wesley's Chapel. *(Boardman preached at John Street. Pilmoor preached for the society in Philadelphia.)*

JB Wakely

CPSIA information can be obtained at www.ICGtesting.com
Printed in the USA
BVOW08s2057020816

457723BV00001B/43/P